PRAISE FOR *INSPIRATION TO REALIZATION*

"This book will inspire you, make you laugh, cry, and most of all, teach you that indeed you can get what you want out of life."
— MARILYN TAM, AUTHOR, *HOW TO USE WHAT YOU'VE GOT TO GET WHAT YOU WANT*

"Finally, gems from the gals on the frontlines. The real nuts, bolts and how-to's for creating the life you want. Thanks ladies!"
— GAYL MURPHY, AUTHOR, *INTERVIEW TACTICS! HOW TO SURVIVE THE MEDIA WITHOUT GETTING CLOBBERED*

"Inside these pages is an abundance of wisdom from dynamic and brilliant women who have poured out the contents of their hearts and heads to provide a power packed tool for success."
— ROBIN FISHER ROFFER, AUTHOR, *MAKE A NAME FOR YOURSELF*

"*Inspiration to Realization* speaks from the heart to women of all ages. Each page is timeless and delivers empowering truths and proven strategies to help women in all areas of their life whether it is business, financial, personal or spiritual. What a wonderful gift given to women by women."
— REBECCA HULEM, "THE MENOPAUSE EXPERT," AUTHOR, *FEELIN' HOT*

"*Inspiration to Realization* will get into your heart and soul and help you to achieve your dreams. Grab it now and sit down for a great read!"
— DEBBIE ALLEN, AUTHOR, *CONFESSIONS OF SHAMELESS SELF PROMOTERS*

"The vision and insight expressed by these women is clear as they share the wisdom present in their personal, business and spiritual lives."
— STEPHANIE FRANK, INTERNATIONAL SPEAKER AND AUTHOR, *THE ACCIDENTAL MILLIONAIRE*

"Women helping women is at the heart of this colorful, common-sense companion for jump starting a career, getting unstuck in a relationship and connecting more deeply with the Wild Divine. An intense understanding of balance between the mental, physical, emotional and spiritual aspects of living is shared by women with unique voices but similar visions."

— SAPPHIRE GRACE, FOUNDER, *EARTH ANGEL PUBLISHING*

"*Inspiration to Realization* is written by real women who have achieved their greatness. After reading this book, I am more motivated to continue with my mission to empower women entrepreneurs. I loved this book and I know that you will too!"

— LINDA HOLLANDER, THE WEALTHY BAG LADY, AUTHOR OF *BAGS TO RICHES: 7 SUCCESS SECRETS FOR WOMEN IN BUSINESS*

"As a mentor and coach, I work with women everyday who clearly express some of the very same concerns that are addressed by the women in this book. While they grow their businesses and expand their wealth how do they get meaningful answers to their questions? What are the time-tested and proven strategies that will help them take action and expedite their goals? How do they find a clear direction that will help them win in the game of life? When readers open the pages of *Inspiration to Realization* they will find all of this and so much more."

— LORAL LANGEMEIR, LIVE OUT LOUD AND WEALTH DIVA

"So many women we know are experiencing challenges with the issues that are addressed in this book. How inspirational to have all of these women as our mentors, or as we would call them, "Earth Angels."

— LORIN AND JERRY BIEDERMAN, AUTHORS, *EARTH ANGELS: TRUE STORIES ABOUT REAL PEOPLE WHO BRING HEAVEN TO EARTH*

"This book shares important messages to help us focus, recharge and reach fulfillment. Messages that we must always remember."
— TASHA NORMAN, PUBLISHER, CEO, *TENDU MAGAZINE*-NYC

"This book proves that we all have greater inner dreams, and those dreams are only able to come into fruition when we follow the path of determination, and the inner faith that within each of us lies as dormant just waiting to be born."
— DONNA M. DOUGLAS, DIRECTOR OF HUMAN RESOURCES, VANSUE INTERNATIONAL GROUP

"This book consists of a collage of real time women who overcame negative mental contamination. Realizing that they possess all power to change their individual circumstances, they are now winners of their personal goals. Even though the testimonials were written by amazing women, I do recommend it to all genders. It will surely inspire you to be victorious."
— WINNIE BENJAMIN, INTERNATIONAL BUSINESS CONSULTANT

"The insight and wisdom in *Inspiration to Realization* is a valuable resource for bringing success into every level of a woman's day to day experience. It's a distillation of shared life lessons from remarkable women that serves as a powerful tool in empowering other women in attaining their dreams. I highly recommend it!"
— ALYSON KAY, AUTHOR, *FRESH OUT OF HELL, ESCAPING THE NEGATIVE INFLUENCES OF TOXIC PARENTING*

"This book is loaded with pearls of wisdom. A terrific guide that gives practical advice and will inspire you to go for your dreams! An eclectic and progressive integration of mind, body, heart and soul. A fabulous addition to your library. A real keeper and great gift for loved ones."
— CHRISSY CAREW, MASTER CERTIFIED COACH

"What you are never taught in school comes through in this book. From start to finish it inspires you to realize your goals and dreams."

— SUE STORM, AUTHOR, THE *ANGEL FIRST AID* SERIES

"Reading this book makes you feel like you are sitting in the center of a circle of women who want to help and support you in their own way. Today's world can be complicated for everyone but especially for women who have so many demands on their time and so many different roles to play.

This book can help you to make sense of it all and give you some down to earth, practical information you can use to make your life more meaningful."

— KRYSTA GIBSON AND RHONDA DICKSION, PUBLISHERS
  AND CO-EDITORS OF *NEW SPIRIT JOURNAL*

"This book is a treasure box of wisdom, inspiration, courage, and transformation from and for women who know they can change the world one woman at a time."

— AGAPI STASSINOPOULOS, AUTHOR, *GODS AND GODDESSES IN LOVE*

INSPIRATION

—— TO ——

REALIZATION

VOLUME II

*This book is dedicated
to all women who march
to the beat of their own drum.*

INSPIRATION

— TO —

REALIZATION

VOLUME II

REAL WOMEN
REVEAL PROVEN
STRATEGIES FOR
PERSONAL, BUSINESS,
FINANCIAL AND
SPIRITUAL
FULFILLMENT

COMPILED BY
CHRISTINE KLOSER

Love
Your   Los Angeles, CA
Life

Published by Love Your Life

PO Box 661274, Los Angeles, CA   90066   USA

Published in the US and Canada by Love Your Life

ISBN: 0-9664806-4-3

Library of Congress Control No: 2004097825

www.LoveYourLife.com

(310) 962-4710

SAN 256-1387

Book Design by Dotti Albertine

CONTENTS

PART III SPIRITUAL FULFILLMENT

Introduction

THANK YOU FOR PICKING UP THIS BOOK! One thing I already know about you is you're a woman with a dream in her heart, and you're willing to do whatever it takes to achieve it!

It has been a great honor to bring together thirty-eight more voices to share in this second volume. Voices of women just like you. They reside all across the United States, and most of them have never met each other, yet they share common goals and dreams. They are the same... and they are different. You'll see they have similar insights, stories and strategies to help you live a fulfilling life, but each with a unique twist.

You may notice this book covers a vast range of topics. The reason? I wanted it to reach women from a variety of backgrounds, ages and varied interests. Just like the women in this book who all have their own journey, I know you have your own unique and powerful journey, too. This book is meant to inspire, motivate, encourage and educate you on your path to realizing your dreams.

In today's fast paced world, it has become even more important to nurture every area of your life—personal, business, financial and spiritual. If you focus on business and forget about your personal or family life, then your business success doesn't have as much meaning. If you only focus on your spiritual life but don't take responsibility for your financial life, then you'll never experience true freedom. This book is about having it all, and it's written by women who want you to have every dream you desire.

How did these particular women come together on this project? They are all members of the Network for Empowering Women Entrepreneurs (www.NEWentrepreneurs.com), a professional association I founded in 2000. The purpose of our journey has been to bring together hearts, souls and minds to create a book that will touch your heart, resonate in your soul and expand your mind.

As you dive into this book, you may choose to read the chapters in order or simply open to a random page and start anywhere. You may find some chapters do not relate to your current situation, yet when you read it twelve months later, the message may be exactly what you need to hear. Let this book be a guide, a resource, and confirmation that you can turn your inspirations into realizations. The women who contributed to this book have all had obstacles to overcome and failures along their way to success. They are ordinary women doing extraordinary things, and if they can achieve their dreams, you can too.

Please share it with a friend, send a copy to your mother, daughter, sister or colleague. The world needs more women who turn their inspirations into realizations. Let your spirit shine and enjoy your journey.

To your success,

Christine Kloser
President, Love Your Life Publishing
Founder, NEW Entrepreneurs, Inc.

PART I

PERSONAL FULFILLMENT

CHAPTER 1

Three Secrets to Living Life Full Out

PAT BACCCILI, Ph.D.

WHAT'S STOPPING YOU?

WE ALL CRAVE PEACE, happiness, health, wealth and prosperity. Why? Because we all have an innate desire to be happy, fulfilled and productive while we express who we really are. We are here for a delicious reason, for we each have a purpose, a sacred quest. We are all innately driven to be happy.

STOP! HALT! TIME OUT!

"You don't really believe that garbage, do you? Listen, Pat, you are from the Bronx. How could you even begin to think that you would get away with believing that you had earned the right to offer that crap to people? Your radio listeners may call you Dr. Pat, but we know who you really are. We were with you all those times that you failed. Get real, Dr. Pat! "

Do any of you recognize a similar voice inside your head telling you that you are not good enough or don't deserve to have what you want? This negative self-talk is your **CRUST** speaking. I know it well, and I know how to shatter this Crust and send it back to the dustbin of history from which it came.

The insidious nature of Crust is that it will always tell you, "No! Don't! You can't!"—even when these limiting comments are not only inappropriate but also not what you want. The truth is that your Crust has nothing to do with who you really are.

What I have discovered in reaching thousands who have moved to the next level of their lives is that they have figured out how to break through their Crust. Today I will share three Crust Busting secrets to help you live life full out.

SECRET #1—LET THE POWER OF YOUR SOUL ROCK YOU

I was born in NYC and lived on the East Coast until a corporate downsizing turned my life "downside up." I had given my all to the company and planned to retire from it. However, I intuitively knew right then that I was at a crossroads in my life and asked myself the question, "Do I sit here and blame the company, my boss and God for the situation, or do I look for the opportunity in it and try something else?" I picked "something else" and by that very choice not to live in the pity of my situation, I began to feel the power of my soul pulling me forward toward a new life. The question was, "Did I have the courage to step out and go after what I wanted in life?"

This was not the first time this question had come up for me. I had always had a dream to be an educator. In fact, many years earlier as a clerk making $61 a week in the mailroom, I turned to my best friend and said, "You know, Linda, I'm going to get a Ph.D!" The truth is that I really didn't know what a Ph.D was. More importantly, for years to come I listened to the voice of limitation, which made a case against my pursuing my dream. However, something was different after the downsizing. I knew that my soul was calling me to a higher purpose and that my life had been rearranged so that I could achieve it. As I sat there in tears only a few years away from retirement, I found the courage to say, "YES! YES! YES!"

I picked myself up and went to graduate school. Somehow, Columbia still had my application on file. A year later, I packed a moving truck, drove across the country and began to do the things I always wanted to do. I was accepted into a Ph.D. program in California, fulfilling a dream I'd had since age twenty-three. Yes, this girl from the Bronx, the first in her family to graduate from high school and the one who took thirteen years to get her undergraduate degree, unleashed the power of her soul to rock her to action.

I realized my soul was trying to get my attention through that downsizing so that all of my talents and all that I am could be used for a purpose greater than myself. I did not have the courage to leave the company on my own. When the door to my old life swung shut, I was faced with the choice of moving forward or being stuck. What I learned was that all I needed to do was turn around to see the many new doors that were open to me to take me to the next level.

Can you recall times when you felt disappointed about a job you did not get? Have you recently gone through a divorce that you thought would end your life? Are you asking yourself, "What is my purpose here?" All of these questions represent challenges you might face in this lifetime. They also represent opportunities for you to let the power of your soul rock you to the next level.

SECRET #2—MINE YOUR MIND

Positive thoughts are like gold. The great thinkers—Herbert Benson, Albert Einstein, Ralph Waldo Emerson, Margaret Mead, Spinoza, Plato, Alice Bailey, Goethe, Ella Wilcox, William James, Eric Butterworth, Leonardo da Vinci, Buckminster Fuller, to name a few—confirm the power of thoughts to transform our lives. Eric Butterworth assures us that "the answer to our success and prosperity is ... in our ability to control our thoughts." Ralph Waldo Emerson told us, "We become what we think about." "Change your thoughts," said Norman Vincent Peale, "and you change the world." "You are the product of your thoughts," as Alice Bailey succinctly put it.

I had the pleasure of interviewing the producers, writers and directors of the movie, "What the Bleep Do We Know?" One of the main messages of the film is that you create your day and thus your reality. Ellen De Generes advised her TV audience to create their day. Drew Barrymore explained to Jay Leno how she created her day. Why do this? In *Your Maximum Mind*, Herbert Benson explains the incredible power of your 10 *billion* plus brain cells as follows:

> "Each of the nerve cells has between 1,000 and 500,000 connections. This means that the number of possible connections is incomprehensibly staggering—something like: 25,000,000,000,000,000,000,000,000,000,000. Put another way, if you stacked upon your desk standard sheets of typing paper, one on top of the other, in an amount equal to the number of possible brain connections, the stack would extend beyond the moon... the planet Pluto... our galaxy... and even beyond the known limits of the entire universe—about 16 billion light years away."

How are you programming your mind through self-talk? Do you jokingly call yourself stupid? Do you use the phrase "Duh" when you think you should have known better? If so, you are programming your brain connections to accept lack and limitation. Choose to mine your mind and select your words and thoughts carefully, just as people like Lance Armstrong have done. Armstrong, winner of seven Tour de France bicycle races, defeated an advanced form of cancer and would not have been able to do what he did if he had not "mined his mind." Similarly, 'O' would simply be a letter in the alphabet had Oprah not believed in the power of her mind.

You are the master of your thoughts, the molder of your health, wealth and prosperity, and the maker and shaper of your destiny. You are a being of power, intelligence and transformation. Tap into the power of your mind and live life full out.

SECRET #3—FIGHT FOR THE TRUTH OF WHO YOU ARE

Do you want to live life full out? Think about this question before you answer. Living full out means going after your dream with steadfast conviction and the unstoppable power of perseverance. It means staying the course despite challenges and rejection. It means believing in miracles and beating the odds. Jack Canfield, co-author of the "Chicken Soup for the Soul" series of books, knows the power of perseverance. During our interview, Jack shared one of the secrets to his success.

"We were turned down with 144 rejections from publishers for "Chicken Soup for the Soul." Our agent gave us our book back after 22 rejections, saying it just wouldn't sell. We went to the American Book Sellers Association and walked the floor booth to booth. We persevered—a success principle. We eventually got a publisher in Florida who no one has ever heard of. The original book went on to sell 8 million copies. I have had a lot of rejection in my life as well as illnesses and death, and I bankrupted my first company. So I learned a lot from experience. You have to believe and not give up."

In search of my Ph.D., all the schools that I applied to rejected me, except one which put me on the waiting list. This meant that I would have to wait a full year at which time there was still no guarantee that I would be admitted. I did not know if I could go through another rejection and almost said no. Right then I knew that this was one of the greatest tests of believing in myself and my dream, which would require persevering in spite of the voice of Crust. I'm not sure exactly how I did it, but I signed the "waiting list" form. Long story short, it is that school where I completed my Ph.D. and went on to win an outstanding research award for my dissertation. I personally learned that you **must** persevere and fight for the truth of who you are.

The truth is that underneath our Crust, each one of us has specific gifts, talents and abilities that are unlike those of anyone else. We have been given them so that we can express ourselves fully and contribute generously to the world around us, in a life lived full out. We only need to bust through our Crust!

DR. PAT BACCILI'S passion to coach people to go after their dreams has catapulted her to syndicated radio. Her listeners call her the "Oprah" of radio. As an award winning researcher, author, consultant and success coach, she uses a unique system to help her clients bust through years of crusty conditioning. Pat's Crust Busting™ breakthrough system uses her "Seven Secrets to Living Life Full Out™." Visit www.crustbusting.com and contact Pat at (206) 523-5533 or at patbaccili@crustbusting.com.

CHAPTER 2

Families Apart
Growing Together

ELIZABETH R. BADER, MAOL

I WAS THIRTY-ONE YEARS OLD standing in the shower, (where I do some of my best thinking), reflecting on the state of my life. The last time my husband and I had been intimate was June 2, 1995. How do I know this? Because that was the day our son was conceived. From that day on, he moved himself into the guest room. It was now early 1997...

We had been to five therapists and a marriage encounter weekend though none of which had moved us any closer; my son had just passed his first birthday, my mother-in-law had just completed her two week visit, (what a fabulous charade that had been), and I was on year two of an empty marriage. I did not like the state of my life. I'd had the good fortune of a few past moments of clarity in my life so I knew how to recognize one when it came. Realizing I was not going to get to where I wanted to be in my life on my current path with my current partner, it was time to go!

So I went!!! I called my parents, told my husband and got a lawyer. By August I was signed, sealed and delivered a single woman and parent; house, cars and money divided.

Two months shy of my thirty-second birthday and mother of an eighteen month old, since I had not worked in three years I needed to quickly figure out some important life decisions. The two most pressing issues that emerged were: raising my child and what was I going to do with me again?

Fortunately the first issue resolved itself quickly and easily. Within weeks of starting the divorce process I had read a horrifying account of a divorce that was so awful and destructive that the author's son chose to walk off the soccer field and not look back. This young boy would rather walk home alone than have to choose between his mother and father camped out at either end of the viewing stands.

I knew as I finished reading that story that would never be me. I vowed right then and there I would do whatever it took to walk the high road and prayed that my son would never be faced with such a choice. What about my ex-husband?

As the universe would have it, some time later standing in the driveway (conducting the first of what would be a long line of transitions for my son), my now ex-husband and I got to talking. I don't remember who brought it up or how, but he came to feel the same way I did. Somehow we agreed, with the raw wounds of divorce still visible, that no one would love our son exactly the way we did, and if we destroy that love, all three of us would be diminished, most especially him. Why couldn't our marriage have been as straight forward?

Seven years later we were given the pearl from the sand we planted in that oyster that day. While visiting his second grade classroom together to view a self-portrait he had painted entitled; "What is important about me." He wrote the following:

"The important thing about me is that my parents love me. I like to play games with my mom and dad. They take me places. I love them. But the important thing about me is my parents love me."

As we stood there in that moment, side by side, reading those words together we smiled. A high five seemed appropriate; hugging was out of the question.

The first pressing issue of the divorce had been addressed. We had tangible proof, at least through the age of seven, that somehow we were doing all right with our son, what about me?

Within weeks of getting divorced I started therapy, I wanted to do whatever I could to learn from this experience and never let it happen again. I also started career counseling because I needed to re-enter the work force. This was big. Since all I ever wanted to be was a wife and mother. I had achieved my life's dream only to have it shattered. Not only was I single again, I now needed to figure out who I was, what I was going to do and remain sane enough to take care of a little person.

I am not sure if it was in the shower this time, however, once again clarity did arrive. What I knew for sure was that since I could not be the stay at home wife and mother of my dreams, I wanted to find a career, not a job, that would give me emotional, spiritual and financial well being. I knew I could not be just an empty cog in a corporate wheel. I wanted to show my son and myself that work could not only provide money, but also a sense of fulfillment and contribution.

Through career counseling I was able to find such a path in Organizational Leadership, specifically training and delivery with an emphasis on leadership and management development. Within six months of the divorce I was in graduate school. Two years later, I received my diploma and got a job.

While the loss of my marriage, the family life I was not able to experience or give to my son weighs on me from time to time, I would never have gained the knowledge that I am a smart, capable person and had something more to offer. As a result of my experiences I founded a company called Positive Co-Parenting to share all that I have learned and help other single parents learn that they can be a family apart and love their children well together and separately.

I sit here today two months shy of my fortieth birthday, my son soon to be ten and eight years divorced. The two big concerns I had after the divorce ironically have now become my life's work. Interesting from a life that comes undone, a person can become more than they ever knew. I still dream about being a family, and I also dream of being a successful businesswoman.

POST SCRIPT

What we know for sure from thousands of pages of research over decades of time is that children who are exposed to continual conflict, that is negatively handled and poorly resolved, experience a multitude of detrimental short term and long term physiological obstacles. They range from low self esteem, poor academic performance, and the inability to emotionally connect, not just at the time of divorce, but as they mature and will possibly be unable to form healthy adult relationships.

Divorce is one of the most challenging and stressful times in life for the adult who is going through it. Imagine being the child…it is possible to grow and evolve as a healthy, well-adjusted person from a divorce, it is possible to love your children well through this time, AND it is possible to learn to be a family apart growing together. It is a choice you can make, for you, for your children and for your former spouse.

ELIZABETH BADER is the founder and creator of POSITIVE CO-PARENTING. She has received a bachelor's degree from Boston University in education, a Masters in Organizational Leadership from Chapman University and a Coaching Certification from the Hudson Institute in Santa Barbara. After spending time in corporate America at companies such as Ingram Micro and Washington Mutual, Elizabeth left to pursue her passion helping divorced parents and their children. Elizabeth enjoys a 100 percent customer satisfaction rate for her one on one coaching. www.positivecoparenting.com.

CHAPTER 3

Three Steps to Courageous Living

TERI HARRISON

You block your dream when you allow your fear to grow bigger than your faith. —MARY MANIN MORRISSEY

I AM NOT NATURALLY FEARLESS. It's just that I refuse to give in to fear. I strive to stretch and improve myself every single day, but I haven't always lived this way. Having spent many years working in the corporate world, creative writing is a relatively new and intimidating experience for me. At first, I was afraid to put these very ideas on paper as part of the initial book application process. But my desire to help and support others is greater than my fear. In pursuit of my dream to be a published author, I decided to harness the energy of my excitement to overpower my anxiety. I now write three to five articles a week as The Business Mom.

By nature, I am a people person and enjoy helping others. Fortunately, I have found my vocation of destiny. As one of the Regional Directors of RBN—Los Angeles County (the Relationship Building Network) I connect entrepreneurs to help them grow their businesses. Within that purpose, I have a more specific passion to support mom entrepreneurs in their quest to juggle business and motherhood.

My husband and I are blessed with two children, Jackie (12) and Cole (4). Like other working mothers, my heart has always been torn, wanting to be with my kids when I was away at work full-time outside the home. What really made the difference was being bitten by the entrepreneurial bug myself and taking the plunge to actually have my own business.

It is important to me that entrepreneurs are able to achieve their dreams, and I want to share three steps that help me live a bold and courageous life filled with faith.

CREATE A NEW PERSONAL VISION

I learned about the need to create a New Personal Vision from the late Dr. Jim Walkenbach. I developed beliefs throughout my life that held me back from living the life I was meant to live. Instead, I lived every day as "Terrified" or "Timid Teri."

Through Dr. Jim's seminar, I took a deep look at myself and discovered my five core values. I also learned that the qualities I admire in others were parts of myself waiting to be expressed. My New Personal Vision created an intention statement for both my personal and professional life—a blueprint of my purpose and mission. I am now "Tremendous Teri." I am grateful to have a greater appreciation for my unique qualities and values. I have a solid foundation from which to pursue my heart's desires, achieve my goals and live with greater integrity. Other members who attended the same seminar became Abundant Anita, Magnificent Mary, Masterful Michael and Successful Susan. You get the idea.

Because of my New Personal Vision, I now live every day with greater courage and confidence that I will achieve my dreams. If you want to build a new and enduring reality, explore your opportunities with a coach or counselor and create your own New

Personal Vision. For more information on how to clarify your five core values and create your own Personal Vision statement, visit www.visionariesuniversity.org.

LIVE A POSITIVE LIFE WITH POSITIVE THINKING AND A POSITIVE ATTITUDE

Positive thinking helps us rise above our fears. We need to spend our days choosing to be happy and creating joy in our conversations. These simple actions will attract the circumstances and events that contribute to our happiness.

In Susan RoAne's "How to Change Your Luck," she writes about having a "you-never-know" attitude. You never know if you don't try; you never know if you don't ask. Good things don't come to us by accident. We need to have a "you-never-know" attitude. Think positively and *ask*. One of the biggest changes I made in my life is not being afraid to ask for an opportunity or the help I need. And my "luck" appears to have changed for the better. Because I recently began asking, I have created new opportunities to be a guest presenter on several teleclasses and to contribute articles to five different publications and websites each month. As I continue to ask, my opportunities continue to increase.

Something else I've learned is when an opportunity presents itself, it is imperative that I act immediately. I don't wait to decide if I think I can do the job. If I wait, I allow my fear a chance to take over. Fears increase when you wait, put off or postpone. Successful people take action.

SURROUND YOURSELF WITH "YOUR PEOPLE"

Through my work expanding RBN, I network throughout the Greater L.A. area meeting hundreds of business professionals every month. Like other entrepreneurs, it has been my experience that not everyone I meet instantly likes me or what I do. It is easy to jump to the conclusion that something is wrong with me, there isn't a need for my particular services, or perhaps I should stop attending networking meetings altogether! Instead, I choose to handle this apparent "rejection" by drawing inspiration from others who have walked in my shoes. Or, as in the case of Chellie Campbell, those who have swam in these waters.

Chellie Campbell, author of "The Wealthy Spirit" teaches that we all swim in the "Ocean of Life" where there are three kinds of fish: Dolphins, Sharks and Tuna. Chellie believes we all need to be as high up on the food chain as possible.

I am so happy when I meet a new Dolphin...
Dolphins are smart and joyful. We need to surround ourselves with Dolphins—the people who like us and encourage us.

I know that you have met a few Tunas in your life...
Tunas are whiners and complainers. They blame things on everyone else. When you meet a Tuna, it is wise to excuse yourself as soon as possible. Be careful not to get caught up into their behavior.

I know that you have met some Sharks, too...
Sharks eat up the whining, complaining Tuna. If you meet a Shark, run! Dolphins can see them head on, but Tunas tend to entangle themselves with Sharks. And you can guess what happens from there...

I will be the first to admit I am a Dolphin who was a Tuna in a previous life! When I was a Tuna, I found myself being surrounded and eaten by Sharks. I was so badly devoured at one point in my life, I am surprised there is anything left of me! I am grateful I learned to change my attitude and view of myself because my life is so much better now.

It is not easy being a Dolphin. It takes great courage warding off Sharks and saving Tuna. But the more I live my life not giving into fear, the more Dolphin I become. Instead of being fearful of other people's opinions, I look forward to meeting "my people"—the people who like me and encourage me—I confidently dismiss others who don't care for me or what I do. If I didn't understand I was on the lookout for "my people," I would have crawled under a big rock long ago worrying about the people who didn't like me. I now know it's impossible to change someone else. We can only model behavior for others. Looking for "your people" can make dramatic difference for you, too.

When you look at yourself in a whole new way, a life filled with courage can be yours. Think positively, encourage opportunities and look for "your people."

TERI HARRISON is The Business Mom. Teri's writing focuses on bringing together the stories and successes of Mom Entrepreneurs to support them in their quest to juggle business and motherhood. To learn how you can contribute to her work, please visit www.thebusinessmom.com. Teri is also one of the Regional Directors of RBN—Los Angeles County (the Relationship Building Network). Visit their website at www.RBNinfo.com. She may be reached at teri@RBNLA.com.

CHAPTER 4

Five Steps to Fulfillment

MARY HEADLEY

OK, SO HERE YOU ARE, ready to get in the car; it's 7:25 am, and you want to get to work by 8:30. First item on your before-work agenda is to drop off child number one who forgot about the special early morning, before-school practice. No problem.

You can make it work since you have to buzz by the post office anyway. The bill for the utility company was due yesterday (it got lost), but they said if it's there tomorrow it'd be all right. It would have been nice to set this all up to pay electronically, but somehow that item keeps getting moved down the "to do" list each month. At least the post office is on the way to school, so if you take the first exit, the dry cleaning will get dropped off too. This will all work out perfectly as long as the traffic cooperates. Today was your morning to meditate from 5:30 to 6:00 am, then spend half an hour on the treadmill, but you didn't hear the alarm. Luckily, the dog insisted on going out so your day started with a wet nose in the face.

If this or something like it has a familiar ring, then you may find yourself like many other women who get to the end of the day feeling frustrated, guilty and emotionally bankrupt. You have been there for everyone except the person who needs the most from you: YOU!

Having six children, completing my bachelor's degree at forty-six while working part-time, and being the only sibling living near my elderly sick parents, I've wrestled with similar issues way too often. Over the past twenty years I've found wise teachers and mentors to guide me. I may not be "super woman," but I am my own woman and much happier with my life. Here are some steps I have used.

LISTING EXERCISE

After spending so much time and energy on others, I lost track of who I was, what I liked, and what talents I enjoyed using for my own joy and satisfaction. I needed to get in touch again with myself, so I purchased a notebook that could be divided into sections. In the first section, using one page for each five-year period of my life, I listed my accomplishments for that time period. Not knowing what you might discover, I recommend just starting at one year old.

At fours years old I was in a "Miss Sunbeam Bread" beauty contest to find a look-a-like for their stylized Miss Sunbeam pictured on the bread package. In the six to ten year old section, I tap-danced to "Here Comes Santa Claus" in a red taffeta dress with white ostrich feather trim. I was the lead in the school Christmas pageant, and started a little "sewing circle" with my friends to make clothes for our dolls.

Each section has its own flavor and surprises. As I looked through my life, I discovered how much I loved some things but never do them or have them around any more. (I was even surprised to find that I could forget such a major accomplishment like handling my mother-in-law's estate for my husband when she died in 1977.) "Oh yeah, I forgot about that," became my mantra. I found it a discovery process worth doing, and there are times I still go back and add to the list.

WEEKEND ON YOUR OWN

Planning and executing this one uses some of our best skills. Imagine thinking of a place you would like to go all by yourself and doing what you like with no interruptions! Do this at least twice a year, maybe tacking it on to a business trip where there is a spa. Inviting a friend is optional.

Guilt was the biggest issue for me when I first started to do these weekends. I've gone to a local hotel with books, music and snacks, utilized room service and rarely went out of the room. Remembering that I always encouraged my friends to take care of themselves—"find some time for yourself"—gave me the determination to do the same for myself. What my family and co-workers got back on the other side was certainly worth the commitment to myself.

GRATITUDE JOURNAL

In your notebook, create a section that you will contribute to each day. My mentor and teacher, Teresa Romaine of Access Abundance, inspired this practice. Here is where you record what you are grateful for having had in your life that day, listing at least five things. As you exercise your gratitude muscle, expand this to ten things per day. It's amazing how much more you will appreciate your life and the people in it. After practicing this, include things you acknowledged yourself for having gotten done that day. The more I recognized, the more this area expanded. In the beginning, making macaroni and cheese or watching "The Simpson's" was the best I could do.

As I started to look for and found evidence that I had lots of conveniences and completions that made my life easier i.e. washing machine/dryer, computer, cell phone, friends and family giving me a hand, school events attended, projects accomplished, dinners made, checkbook balanced, I woke up happier and stayed that way into my day. There are plenty of references in Scripture and other sacred texts to the bounty available to each of us. Perhaps looking for it is all that's required to experience it.

GIVE YOURSELF PERMISSION TO DREAM

This idea of dreaming and actually having my dreams come true was something I thought only happened in Disney features. Of course I've wanted things and gotten them, but my experience was that BIG dreaming wasn't practical, affordable or in everyone's best interest. There were always home improvements, car repairs, braces and vet bills lining up for financial resources. That month-long trip to Italy or cruise in the Mediterranean would have to wait for after (fill in the blank) _____ happened. Think of some of the dreams you've crossed off your list. Consider whether you think you deserve it, even if you have the time and money.

Sonja Choquette in her book "You Heart's Desire" gave me a new experience of dreaming. Following the steps she describes brought back the child-like part of me that finds the world amazing and my own desires worthwhile. We are never too old, and it's never too late to answer our Heart's calling.

WEEKLY DATE WITH YOURSELF

The last thing you might think about doing is going on a date with yourself. I promise there are fewer conflicts in this event. Who will you argue with? Whose turn is it to pick the movie, you or you? You've always wanted to stop by that little store that sells antique teapots but no one else is interested. So?! Here's your chance. Do whatever you want for at least an hour once a week. You might be thinking this is too hard, or "I can't find time for that!" Are you sure?

I have gone to a spice store to see what's there, looked at tiles just to see what's new, zipped into a matinee during the middle of the week, gone to a jewelry store pretending to shop for a dinner ring, sat by the lake watching the ducks, taken a drive down a country road I'd always wanted to explore. The freedom is wonderful!

Give these steps a try. Give it three months. We certainly deserve to treat ourselves as well as we treat others. You may find that the mad dash on Monday is nothing because Wednesday evening is all YOURS, and you can't wait!

MARY HEADLEY is a mother of six and currently living with two sons in rural Wisconsin. She writes, designs and delivers workshops that empower creativity and self-expression. Using her training in Feng Shui, coaching, teaching, and psychic abilities, her consulting practice assists her clients in unblocking energy in their environment and life. She can be reached via email at: mary@maryheadley.com for private consultation, coaching, information, or to schedule a workshop.

CHAPTER 5

Loving the Life
I Never Knew I Wanted

NICKI HESKIN

I NEVER KNEW I wanted to be an entrepreneur. In fact, while I most certainly have the life I want, I can't say truthfully that I have the life I always wanted—because I never knew it existed. In my past life, I ran events, alumni programs and fundraising efforts for universities and secondary schools. Before my daughter was born, I always just assumed I'd be a full-time working mom because I couldn't imagine that there was any other way we could live. I went on maternity leave in October with plans to be back in April.

After the sleep deprivation and breastfeeding challenges of the first few months had passed and I finally began to revel in day-to-day motherhood and love for my daughter, Jenna, I found myself in complete denial as my return day to work grew closer. I sat down for a meeting with my boss to talk about job sharing, part-time or contract work and walked away feeling like I might be able to "have it all." However, when she met with the headmaster of the school, this otherwise progressive leader flatly refused such an arrangement and sent a letter informing me I was required to return to work on the day we had arranged or resign.

I was shattered. I was terrified about how we'd make the money work, and my sense of value as a professional vanished. But after long "strategy sessions" with my very supportive husband and much soul searching, we let our newly formed parental instincts guide us down the only path we knew we could take, and I became unemployed for the first time since I was fourteen years old.

Once the initial shock wore off, I discovered that for the first time in my life I was doing exactly what I wanted to be doing! While I had loved my career and was great at it, I had never really chosen it. Like many adults, my professional life had somehow unfolded over the years, and I continued down the path because I had never been inclined or forced to explore any detours or scenic routes along the way.

So for a relatively blissful year, I found a whole new life. I gloried in my daughter's babbles, snuggles and small accomplishments. I discovered parks and library story times. I made new friends and planned play dates. The money somehow took care of itself with a refinance and a raise for my husband. I couldn't imagine a life I could love more.

When Jenna was fifteen months old, we were offered a rare spot in the Infant Development Program (IDP) at UCLA, for which we had joined the waiting list while I was pregnant and still planning to go back to work. Although we loved how things were going, the program was so incredible that we decided to try it two days a week.

For a second time, an unexpected change affected our lives in wonderful ways we could have never imagined. The influence of IDP on our lives cannot be measured. We always knew we wanted to parent our daughter in a respectful and natural way, but IDP showed us what this sort of parenting could tangibly LOOK like— what to do and what to say to bring our vision in line with the day-to-day realities of parenting. Her caregivers exposed us to parenting philosophies and techniques that we might not have discovered on our own, and we became better parents for sharing our daughter with them. IDP also allowed me to begin to emerge from the "mommy-cave" I had been in and start to look around at what I could be doing with my two "found" days each week. Finally, it started me thinking about great parenting as a learned skill, not just a process of fumbling down a path paved with love and good intentions.

After attending IDP with Jenna while she got adjusted, catching up on errands, finishing some deferred condo projects, and finding a new yoga class (which I'd been missing desperately since my daughter's birth!), I realized that I'd better find something worthwhile to do while Jenna was at IDP. So I turned to Craigslist.com, that Internet vortex of odd jobs, virtual work and interesting opportunities, where I thought I might find something that would fill my time and help pay for Jenna's very expensive daycare program. Somewhere among the varied junk, full-time jobs, scams and mismatches, one item shined through:

> "Part Time Virtual Administrative/Office Assistant—I own a small, but growing business that helps educate, empower and inspire women entrepreneurs to start a business, grow a business and turn their dreams into reality. I can't do it on my own anymore and need a 'right hand person' who will effectively and joyously handle the operations of my business."

This job posting was by Christine Kloser, the founder and executive director of NEW Entrepreneurs, Inc. and the publisher of this book. I checked out the NEW website and quickly responded with a short, authentic statement of my background and circumstances and my admiration for and interest in her mission and vision. Given the nature of many items on Craigslist, I would not have been surprised to have never heard anything about it again.

What I now recognize as the Universe was again looking out for me and guiding me down a path I couldn't yet see. My response apparently spoke to Christine in much the same way that her listing spoke to me, and among the hundreds of responses she received, we made a connection. After meeting Christine, she encouraged me to attend a NEW meeting to see if it felt right. After my first meeting (similar to the experience of many NEW members, I'm told), I was hooked! I had never seen myself as very spiritually centered, but I knew somehow this was something I needed to do.

I started out working only about five hours a week for Christine and attending meetings to help out. I found myself becoming spiritually more awake and finding comfort in the love, energy and integrity of the women I met each month. My "NEW" professional life took me down a path that made my increasingly more natural parenting choices and experiences resonate even more clearly and confidently. And I began to see my experiences, especially my parenting journey, as something of value that could help others find what I had been lucky enough to stumble upon. Slowly I began to think like these entrepreneurial women I had come to admire.

I was lucky to have Christine's patience, understanding and support over the next many months as she shared me with another part-time job, followed by a new job for my husband, a condo sale, a house purchase (yay!), the inevitable move that goes along with all of that, a farewell to the beloved IDP program for Jenna and a transition to a new, also great, preschool. In the midst of this, the Universe continued to watch over my journey. Just as I was finally able and ready to commit more to NEW, Christine was readying herself for her own new path of motherhood. My resulting increased involvement in NEW turned my part-time inspiration into a real career—one I never knew I could have from home in my jammies— or in arms reach of my daughter!

And finally, after a year of joking at NEW meetings that I was the only woman in the room without a business of her own, I am slowly stepping out with my own venture—to bring to other mothers the same sorts of resources I was lucky enough to find as a parent and a professional—www.learnedparenting.com. I don't yet know how it will actually make me any money, but I trust in the Universe to continue to lead me toward choices that will make sense of it all, and let the rest follow naturally.

One thing I know now is that I will never work in a traditional office again. Women CAN have it all, and on our own terms. If you had told me when I graduated high school that in fifteen years I'd own a house, have an amazing marriage, a wonderful daughter, work part-time at home for a full-time salary, be a published author and starting my own business, I would have never believed you.

But on I go, loving the life I never knew I wanted...

NICKI HESKIN is the member services director of NEW Entrepreneurs, Inc. (www.newentrepreneurs.com) and the owner of the website www.Learned Parenting.com. As of late 2005, this Internet-Based Parenting Resource Center is still in development, but watch for great things to come! She is accepting ongoing submissions for content and resource suggestions to make this site as valuable as possible for parents. Check back at www.LearnedParenting.com for current contact information or reach her at nh@newentrepreneurs.com.

CHAPTER 6

Relationship 101:

How to Survive
a Healthy Relationship

SHERRI HUGHES SOKOL, C.Ht.

A HAPPY, HEALTHY RELATIONSHIP with a significant other is a true gift of life though keeping it that way can sometimes be a struggle. Time seems to challenge the best of relationships through familiarity, lack of interest, family obligations or just simply growing apart. By means of personal trial and error and the wonderful voices of my clients and colleagues, I have been gathering information about what it takes to maintain a healthy, loving, meaningful relationship. Below are thoughts on how to successfully survive a happy relationship:

TEN WAYS TO MAINTAIN A HEALTHY RELATIONSHIP:

1. *Purposeful communication is essential.* Take the time to create a space for revealing ourselves and being intimate without fear or judgment. Being able to reveal who we are and what we want in a safe environment is a wonderful sign of a healthy relationship. Communicate with the intent to understand first, then to be understood and with the idea to leave both parties empowered.

Whenever I think I'm right about something and someone is wrong, then I've already lost. I've discovered wrongs and rights divide relationships and cut off the opportunity for individual and couple growth.

2. *Forgiveness* is one of the greatest tools to use in creating a bond between two people; it is an opportunity to operate out of unconditional love, learn from the experience and then move on. Holding onto past hurts and negative energy will kill the joy in a relationship quickly. Forgiving ourselves is often the best place to start.

    Sometimes to practice forgiveness means not taking myself so seriously and looking first at my own shortcomings in the situation. What I dislike in my partner is almost always what I dislike in myself. It is amazing how people show up in our lives to offer mirrors so we see ourselves and then give us another opportunity to get it right. If my partner is pushing buttons then I can be grateful for the opportunity to discover more about myself.

3. *Have fun.* Finding common interests and goals is very significant in a healthy relationship. Providing opportunities for playfulness, learning new things together and creating common interests are great ways to provide passion for life and in the relationship. Laughing together and having fun is great therapy.

    Having fun also means having an active, fulfilling sex life. Enjoying each other on this intimate level provides a level of closeness that is not shared with others and makes this relationship special. This also includes not using sex and affection as a tool to harm a partner by withholding or seeking intimacy outside of the relationship.

4. *Develop a spiritual life together* and understand that there is a higher presence in control, and neither one of you are it. It is

important to surrender ourselves and the relationship to true source and allow life to unfold in a natural grace according to a divine plan.

Time spent together in prayer, meditation and reflection is a wonderful foundation for a life together. Being on equal spiritual grounds with similar beliefs is valuable in creating an atmosphere of common goals and interests. It is said that a couple who prays together, stays together.

5. *Honor the differences* between being male and being female and allow each other to be of equal value and importance. Men and women are just different! Isn't that the good news! Let's quit making the other sex wrong for thinking and behaving differently than ourselves and respect and appreciate each other for the uniqueness we can contribute to the relationship. Looking past our differences and valuing our similarities is a great playing field and lessens the separateness we get when we're comparing one another.

6. *Be your partner's best cheerleader,* offer support in the day-to-day struggles and celebrate the joys of everyday life. Being present emotionally and physically is very important in honoring your partner. If there is a particular area of concern or interest for the other person which requires your support then it is vital to the relationship to show up and be available. Assisting each other to stretch and grow in ways that we couldn't on our own is very valuable and certainly makes life more rewarding. The synergistic effect is true in relationships; two working together can summon more energy and co-create more than each partner acting on their own.

7. *Trust and honesty* are one of those givens in a relationship, though it is important to note that honesty is much more than telling the truth. Honesty is revealing fully who we are, first

with our self and then with another, without fear of judgment, embarrassment or shame. Also, knowing what is not said is just as significant as what is said. Withholding feelings, emotions and information is a game played without any winners.

True honesty comes from keeping our word and being authentic in our self-expression, which creates trust in each other and honors the relationship. To have a relationship of trust, we must operate in an attitude of unconditional love and total acceptance.

8. *Maintain self-identity* by making efforts every day to add quality to your life outside of your relationship. It is good to stay involved with friends and have other personal interests outside of the relationship. Remember, to thine own self be true—keep yourself fit inside and out for your own well-being. This simple act validates our importance as an individual, increases our self-confidence and high self-esteem and is very attractive to others. When we feel in our power as an individual, then we are capable of being an effective partner in the relationship and can come together out of abundance and desire instead of need.

   It is also a good idea to be as financially self-supporting as possible for your situation. This gives each partner the freedom to make his/her own decisions and prevents any one from feeling undervalued or over worked. Money has power, so remember to honor its value while maintaining some financial independence from your partner. This level of self-responsibility is also important for personal growth and success in life.

9. *View the relationship itself as a separate entity* from you as individuals and make decisions based on its higher good. Make the relationship important and find ways to nourish, feed it and to create opportunities to enhance intimacy both emotionally and physically. Striving to work toward common goals, rather than

individual goals, with loving self-sacrifice not self-deprivation, is a certain way to develop a strong, loving relationship that can sustain the test of time and provide joy.

10. *Take personal responsibility* for what you want from the relationship and from life. It is up to you to do your own work and make life better for you and the relationship. Rarely can another person live up to our ideals nor can we live up to theirs. High expectations of others are resentments waiting to happen, so keep expectations low and acceptance high, knowing that the only person we can truly change is ourself and all change truly begins from within.

Too often we look outside of ourselves for solutions to improve our own lives and hold others responsible for our unhappiness. As Gandhi says, be the change you want to see in others.

In closing, enjoying the relationship you are in is not as much about the other person as about you. You can only love another to the extent you love yourself, and you can only allow someone else to love you to the extent you love yourself. Loving yourself first is the greatest gift you can give to you, your partner and to the relationship. Love yourself, love others and enjoy.

SHERRI HUGHES SOKOL, C. HT utilizes a unique combination of Life Coaching, Hypnotherapy and Reiki to assist clients in transforming their life and relationships. She offers valuable insights and tools in recognizing and eliminating negative blocks to the joy and full potential of life. Sherri is available for a complimentary personal consultation by phone (919) 272-1454 and E-mail: Sherrihs@aol.com and offers empowering group presentations on the Power of Thoughts and Beliefs and Relationship Recovery and Skills. View additional writings and CDs at: www.sherrisokol.com.

CHAPTER 7

From Resolution to Reality:

How to Stay Fit and Lose Fat Forever!

ANITA KUGLER

YOU'VE HEARD THE SCARY HEADLINES. You know about heart disease and diabetes, and you know that this is the year you're really going to do something to improve your health. You've written out your New Year's resolutions and your fitness goals, and you've posted them prominently on your bathroom mirror, next to your computer, and on the door of your refrigerator.

Fast forward to the middle of March. Where do you see yourself? Did you stick to your plan? Are you meeting your goals? Are you frustrated? Did you lose some weight and then gain it back? Are you resigned to just do your best for the moment and start all over again right around Memorial Day?

What if there were an easier way? What if you could use a simple, health-promoting, permanent fat-loss formula to guide your daily actions that was so effective, and so easy to follow, that you would never have to make that resolution again, for the rest of your life?

That formula really does exist!

Imagine connecting all of your separate fitness "dots" and seeing them as components of a single, whole, healthier lifestyle. Imagine bringing those aspects of your life into balance in such a way that after a few months, you're exercising, you're eating well, you feel great, you've lost a few inches here and there, and you look fabulous! You're hardly even thinking about it anymore, because it's just become a part of who you are and what you do.

When I was looking for a way to bring all of my fitness goals together, I found a program that really works. It's called "Healthy for Life" and it was developed by Ray D. Strand, M.D., who has practiced medicine for more than thirty years and written several books on nutrition and health. Dr. Strand tested this concept with his own patients for more than ten years. What he discovered was that by helping people "connect the dots," many chronic illnesses, including chronic weight management problems, could be permanently reversed.

Diet is critical. Exercise helps. Supplements are beneficial. But it's only when we combine all three that we greatly improve our chances of successfully losing weight and becoming healthier in the process. Many popular weight loss systems focus only on one of these elements, or on two, but in the "Healthy for Life" program, all three elements are equally important.

FOOD: IT'S ALL ABOUT BLOOD SUGAR

Our bodies require sugar (glucose) to function, so the food we eat is broken down, and some of it becomes sugar. Some foods raise our blood sugar very quickly, while other foods break down more slowly, giving our bodies a steady, continuous source of energy.

"Spiking" our blood sugar causes big problems. When there's more sugar in the blood than the body needs, the body looks for places to store the excess sugar. It's not like drinking too much caffeine, which passes through our system and wears off after a while. It's more like filling up your garage with extra stuff, little by little, until one day the idea of getting rid of it all is too overwhelming, so you figure out ways to rearrange everything to fit more stuff in.

This may sound overly simple, but when we're trying to lose weight, excess sugar in our blood is our biggest enemy.

Here are just a few examples of how we can avoid spiking our blood sugar:

- Avoid foods that get converted to sugar very quickly, such as white bread, bagels, white potatoes, white rice, raisins, processed juices, popcorn, and many popular breakfast cereals. Replacements could include breads made with whole or sprouted grains, brown or basmati rice, whole fruits, and bran cereals. You may not like broccoli, but you can healthfully replace white potatoes with just about any vegetable you can think of, including squash, yams, carrots and peas.

- Eat balanced meals and snacks. Balance protein, carbohydrates and fats—we need all of them, and quality is more important than quantity. For protein, replace fatty or highly processed meats with turkey, chicken, nuts, soy products, beans, fish and low-fat dairy. Eliminate hydrogenated oils and deep fried foods; use virgin olive oil, nuts and avocados as sources of fat.

- Eat three meals and two or more healthy snacks every day. Eating frequently means you can make healthier food choices and still never be hungry! This really works! If you allow yourself to become too hungry, you are very likely to overeat at your next meal. Eating frequently helps to keep your blood sugar level, your overall energy level, and your mental alertness even throughout the day.

EXERCISE: A LITTLE GOES A LONG WAY

The fact that exercise is an important element of any weight loss program is certainly not news. But the reason may have nothing to do with "burning calories." It turns out that exercise helps our body to balance out our blood sugar levels.

Many people find that walking is the easiest form of exercise to incorporate into their day. And yes, getting in a few minutes of walking by parking at the far end of the parking lot when you go to the supermarket, the mall or the movies does count! Some of us need other forms of exercise as well to get the shaping, toning and conditioning we desire.

Whatever you choose, be sure to start slowly if you haven't been exercising recently, and gradually build up to doing some form of exercise for 20 to 30 minutes five days a week. Consistency is the key. That four-hour hike on the weekend may be a wonderful way to relax, but to really experience the long-term benefits of exercise, add something that you enjoy doing that fits into your normal schedule throughout the week.

SUPPLEMENTS: KEEPING YOUR CELLS HAPPY

If you're a gardener, or even if you've only got a houseplant or two, you know that your plants need certain things to stay healthy. Plants can't tell us what they like to eat, so we have to figure out what their nutritional needs are. Most need nutritional "supplements" to remain healthy. Even organic growers use soil supplements to ensure the best possible nutritional balance for their crops.

These "supplements" are not designed to help the plant get thinner! Their purpose is simply to nourish the cells so that the plant will be healthy and strong. Healthy plants not only look more beautiful, but they also resist diseases more easily.

As human beings with complex bodies and trillions of cells, we also need nutritional supplements to stay healthy, look good and resist disease. Scientists tell us that even a healthy diet doesn't provide us with all the nutrients we need.

Supplements that balance a wide variety of vitamins and minerals in optimal doses keep our cells in optimal condition. When our cells are nourished and satisfied throughout the day, we won't be bothered by hunger pangs and cravings.

Think of supplements as a way of giving your body a nice treat while you turn your attention to improving your diet and finding the time to exercise!

IT WORKS IF YOU STAY WITH IT!

It takes time to develop new habits. Remember to be kind to yourself as you watch your new lifestyle evolve.

Will you stay motivated? Will you keep your focus throughout the year? The "Healthy for Life" program can help you with daily tips, an online journal and ongoing support for your healthy lifestyle choices.

Enjoy the process of discovering new ways to eat and exercise. Share your journey with friends and family members who may also benefit from this program.

Have fun, and remember that your resolution really can become a reality!

ANITA KUGLER is passionate about helping people improve their health. For more than thirty years, she has researched and explored many approaches to living a healthy lifestyle. She is a writer, an educator and a Certified Team Leader for the "Healthy for Life" program. For helpful tips, free downloadable articles and a free subscription to her monthly newsletter, visit her website: www.TrueHealthNetwork.com. For questions and more information, contact her by email: anita @TrueHealthNetwork.com, or by phone: (818) 735-8862.

CHAPTER 8

Navigating the Frog Pond

SALLY LANDAU

IF SINGLE WOMEN WILL GET OUT OF THEIR OWN WAY, they can forge a path into successful dating.

Okay, so you're twenty-five, burned out by late night partying and Monday hangovers. You're in your mid-thirties, have had some long-term relationships, your fill of blind dates, and more than enough of the bar scene. Or maybe you're in your forties and, sadly, the men you meet are looking for bright, fresh-faced twentysomethings.

Your fifties bring new questions. You had the married life experience, the divorce dilemma, and you've sneaked a peak at Internet dating and are too scared to post a profile, much less a photo. The men you meet are lame and soft as declawed house cats. Do any men still have testosterone coursing through their veins?

After sixty, you think Internet dating is amusing and are wondering if any of the men reading your profile have a GED or have begun shaving. You don't know whether to be flattered or be horrified by their invitations, "Wanna play?"

It doesn't matter in which decade you find yourself. The universal theme among unsatisfied, single women remains constant: Are all the good ones taken?

When dating is drudgery or seems a lost cause, a lot of women make decisions to hunker down and concentrate on their careers. Or they find respite in the comfort of their female friends, who provide continuity, little criticism, laughter, love, genuine concern, intellectual stimulus, positive energy....almost everything we want in a man, except sex.

Other women, injured by a former relationship, either attract even worse men than they've known previously or write off the entire gender, holing up in their homes with books, TV or knitting. Some have six cats.

On the other hand, there are many women who are completely satisfied being single. Their lives are full, exciting and fun. They either never have or never want again to share a bathroom, closet, bed or refrigerator with a man, and life is just ducky that way. This chapter is not talking to them.

You only have to look at dating websites to see that there are lots of men out there looking, and mostly they're available... legally and emotionally. According to the 2000 US Census for women through age sixty-four, there are more than nine men for every ten women. Through age eighty-four, the numbers drop only to seven for every ten.

So why is it that so many women share the cry that the good ones are taken? Why do they give up? As a life coach, I encourage my clients to proceed toward the achievement of goals they have not been able to realize on their own. There are really just a few reasons people do not achieve their dreams. Many give up too quickly. Many never begin the work and others just need someone to hold their hand through those times when they otherwise would quit.

Dating successfully isn't any different.

My grandmother probably would have said, "Sweetie, men are not coming in over the transom." This just means we have to be proactive.

First, you'll have to prioritize your time and money. You can devote funds to a myriad of things, but you have to choose—appearance, wardrobe, e-mail and cell phone for security reasons, monthly website subscriptions, dating events, etc.

Wonderful, available men are everywhere. We just have to know how to find them. The truth is, they're in all the usual places. Internet dating can and has proven itself successful. Many of us know more than one person who has found the love of their life in cyberspace. There are speed or rapid dating events. Matchmakers (good ones, anyway) can help couples find love. Personal ads. The bars are still there; just make sure you go with a friend, or take a "wingman." There are bookstores and libraries, Sierra Club hikes, cycling clubs, art galleries and museums, ball games, hardware stores, horse and auto races. There are also organizational activities of like interests, travel and cruises. There are hundreds of places to meet men, but you've got to make the effort.

The fact is, you can meet him across a crowded room, in an elevator, in your doctor's waiting room. He's out there, and here's a news flash—he's looking too! And you don't have to do much. A warm, toothy grin can break the ice. "Hello, ride this elevator much?" begins a chat.

Remember to quiet the critical inner voice. Here are a few stories I've heard about men who were given a second chance: A man who cares deeply about his appearance just one day buttoned his shirt lopsided and looked like a geek. A woman who demands a clean-shaven face met a wonderful (but scruffy) man who had just suffered a thirty-six-hour plane delay from a private meeting with the Dalai Lama. Another had a job my client perceived below her in the professional chain, but he reads ancient Greek, speaks twelve languages, has traveled the world, is a gourmet cook and gives an expert massage.

I hear from too many men that they find women intimidating. They are afraid to make the first move. They've been blasted by accusations that they've come on to women when all they offered was a hello. They've found women angry because "my last man did me wrong." The baggage some women bring to the first date could not be stuffed into a steamer trunk. (Hey, this is not an exclusively female trait!) To climb the corporate ladder, a lot of women have adopted a ball busting approach that they forget to leave at the office when they enter the coffee house. Or their "women's agenda" enters the room before they do.

Successful dating and eliminating the frogs is easy. We need to be in the moment, open to what might come next, not worrying about how what we say might be judged. If we approach dating as an opportunity to learn more about ourselves and focus less on "Gee, will he like me?" we'll get more out of dating…and a whole lot better at it.

As with most things, we find that experience makes us more comfortable in our skin, more confident in our delivery, and more natural in every way. Men are looking for real women. We also become more familiar with our boundaries and when they are crossed. In other words, we see the curve ball coming sooner and know when not to swing the bat.

It's obvious we need to like ourselves before we can expect to be liked by others, and therefore, successful at dating. This may be more challenging for some than others. Dating a lot is like rehearsing for a play or practicing a sport—the more you do it, the better you get at it.

Then there are those who postpone dating, because they've created an artificial barrier: I need to lose fifteen pounds. I should be working out at the gym more regularly. I need to have a more impressive job, a better apartment, a newer car. We can wait and we can wait and we can wait. Who was that smart person who said, "Tomorrow never comes, because it's always today?"

Dating will begin the day you decide you're ready. When you know what you're looking for, know what turns you on, are aware of your boundaries and willing to withhold snap judgments, you become the magnet for the anti-frog. He's out there. Go find him.

SALLY LANDAU dated forty-six quality men inside of six months. This intense experience taught her many lessons about successful dating and resulted in a continuing two-year relationship with her partner, Ken. As a life coach, she helps women and men who think dating is drudgery and a no-win journey, by turning them onto a new path leading toward renewed hope and success. You can reach her at (310) 780-0966 or www.sallylandau.com.

⌒

CHAPTER 9

Finding your Rhythm and Balance through Animal Wisdom

RENEE MCDUFFY

EVER BEEN SICK WITH THE FLU OR A COLD? Perhaps you've had surgery and spent time in bed at home recovering? Did your pets find their way to your bedside? Probably they did. Perhaps they even camped out near your surgical site or on your chest.

When we are sick, our pets help us rediscover our personal rhythm, which accelerates our healing. With all we do as entrepreneurs, mothers, wives, sisters, friends and daughters, it can be easy to lose track of who we are and be shaken out of our true rhythm. We may even lose connection with Source (God, Buddha, Creator) and cause illness in our bodies.

This lack of balance with our personal rhythm causes havoc— not only with our bodies but with our emotions, too. Our emotional health is the foundation for our physical health as well as our sense of well-being. Neglecting this fundamental life force can show up in ways that affect the whole of who we are, including our business success. Our relationships with our beloved pets often mirror how we face the world and what we manifest in it.

Take Carolyn, a young entrepreneur, who found an expanded and more affirming sense of herself by taking a deeper look at her relationship with her terrier, Sparky.

Carolyn called one day because Sparky had been suffering for some time with severe allergy symptoms which included itchy, scaly skin and sores where she had scratched herself raw. Very little fur remained.

Carolyn had taken Sparky to multiple vets (holistic and traditional), had tried home remedies and over-the-counter remedies to no avail. Some of the treatments worked for a time, but then the symptoms would recur. Carolyn was at her wits end, watching this beloved dog suffer.

Carolyn came to me to hear Sparky's input. My job as an animal whisperer is to listen to the wisdom of our animals and form a communication bridge by opening up these important relationships to the love and wisdom that sources them.

A conversation with Sparky revealed that she was mourning the passing of Carolyn's husband. Carolyn explained that she was also mourning but always expressed herself in private. She wanted to protect Sparky because she knew how attached Sparky had been to her deceased husband.

She went on to say how Sparky lay curled up on his pillow for weeks after his passing crying, whimpering and wailing. Carolyn did everything she could to console Sparky; she encouraged her to eat, go for walks and be a dog again. Sparky wouldn't budge.

It became clear, through my chat with Sparky, that Carolyn's next step was to begin to express her grief in front of her little dog. She could indicate if she wanted to cry and use Sparky as her pillow. If Carolyn felt sad, she could sit and be sad with Sparky. And if she was angry because her husband was not there to hang the pictures in her new home (because that was his job when they had moved in the past), she could tell Sparky exactly how she felt.

Carolyn saw the wisdom in these suggestions and agreed to try them.

Four months later, Carolyn told me Sparky's condition had dramatically improved. The itching had stopped, the skin had healed, and the fur had grown back healthier than ever. Best of all, Sparky's personality had returned to her spunky, curious and loving nature, albeit much wiser for the experience.

Carolyn noted her own approach to life had changed considerably. As she shared her emotions and joined her dog in sorrow, she was able to lift a veil of emotion she hadn't realized was there.

As her dog's body recovered and their emotions healed, darkness lifted, and joie-de-vivre returned to both of them.

This is when Carolyn really began to shine. As she went into the world, she brought with her an energy that others found very warm, welcoming and loving.

As a result, her struggling business blossomed and took on new life. Her friendships were renewed on a much healthier level. She experienced contentment within as she shared her time, love and energy with Sparky, while conducting business and being a woman living a life she truly loved.

While Carolyn certainly meant well when she tried to protect Sparky, she hadn't realized she was hampering Sparky's healing as well as her own.

Freeing up the emotions so deeply locked into that tragic event allowed physical, emotional and spiritual healing for both of them. It allowed Carolyn the freedom to live life more fully and expand her business and personal life. It also gave Sparky freedom to become more active in life and express herself.

Conversations with our animals empower us to see a way to the truth that had eluded us. Utilizing this loving and compassionate connection has helped many open to spiritual growth through the wisdom, kindness, compassion and love ever present in our pets.

I do not claim to cure illness; in this case, when the vet's expertise did not produce the desired results, Sparky's symptoms clearly presented as an emotional issue, for which the vets simply are not trained.

Sparky and Carolyn actually healed themselves by opening to spiritual growth and expansion, accessing the emotions they had kept bottled up inside, looking at them head-on and then being willing to face them together.

This is the synergy behind the work I do. It usually begins with a request to address a problem and ends up revealing something very powerful and enriching to both the animal and the human.

What are you holding onto that might be showing up in your pet?

Is your bird plucking out his feathers? Perhaps you're feeling particularly anxious about an upcoming event or deadline.

Is your horse throwing her riders? Perhaps you are harboring anger that you have resisted addressing.

We all have the ability to tune in to our pets and get a sense of what they are feeling, which may show up as self-destructive or other negative behavior.

Keep in mind we do not cause our pets to experience these emotions or negative behaviors. They came with their own set of "stuff" that... hmm... coincidentally mirrors our "stuff."

If you notice your pet is not doing well or is doing something unusual, possibly destructive, she may be asking for your attention to address something you may have overlooked in the busy-ness of life.

Take a moment to tune in. Get a feel for the energy of your pet and ask: What is the emotion behind this action?

Then ask: Is there anything here that applies to me? It's likely there is something here for you.

Checking in with your emotions may pave the way for your pet's communication to be more effective.

Including your pet in your emotional life puts you more in tune with your own personal rhythm and helps the body, mind and feelings to stay in balance. It also produces a deeper level of respect, understanding and relating to your pet, leading to greater abundance in all aspects of life.

Connect with your pet. Watch for the reflections of those parts of yourself that get ignored as you strive to succeed in life. This will help you find your rhythm and balance. It will also help heal emotional and physical ills that could be getting in the way of having what you truly want.

And I can't imagine a kinder, gentler, more loving and fun way than through the wisdom of animals.

ANIMAL WHISPERER RENEE MCDUFFY speaks with animals. She assists in getting to the heart of an issue through gentle, open conversations. This creates deeper animal/person relationships. It reveals solutions to issues and empowers us with truth. Renee services clients internationally and is available to speak to your group and write articles for your publication. For a FREE report titled "The First 3 Steps to Communicating with your Pet" go to www.renee4animals.com or call Renee at (949) 495-8864.

CHAPTER 10

Aging is an Inside Job
BARBARA C. PHILLIPS, NP

ARE YOU TIRED OF SEEING BLACK BALLOONS and over-the-hill-merchandise at birthday celebrations? Many women are. They want to celebrate, not hold a wake!

It's no secret; within the next five years, there will be an estimated 41.2 million women over the age of 45 in the U.S. alone. Happily, this generation of women wants a different aging experience.

Women are bombarded daily with anti-aging messages such as getting rid of wrinkles and covering gray hair. While we all want to look as good and be as healthy as the next woman, aging is about so much more.

Many women do not realize the different ways in which we age. While we don't have direct control over the number of years we live, we can directly impact our experience of aging through attitude, health, and purposeful life experiences.

WHAT ARE SOME DIFFERENT WAYS OF AGING?

CHRONOLOGICAL AGING

You know that number. You see it on your driver's license and birthday cake. That is our chronological age—the number of years we have been living.

Luxie, a delightful nine year old, recently told me she would "finally get to be a double digit" this year. Obviously, she is looking forward to her tenth birthday. Shouldn't we all be excited about our next birthday?

BIOLOGICAL AGING

Biological age has to do with what's going on inside the body. While genetics play a role, you can have a major impact on your biological age and health by means of nutrition, exercise, environmental issues, toxins, chemical exposure and more. Your goal is to maximize the quality of your health, thus enhancing your chronological and experiential age.

EXPERIENTIAL AGING

How much living have you done thus far in your life? Have you tried new activities or exposed yourself to new ideas, cultures, and foods? The more "living" you do translates into many years of life experiences.

WHAT YOU CAN DO

To maximize your age and enhance the quality of your life, there are several things you can do to insure your life remains vibrant and healthy. While these are in separate areas, they need to be viewed and acted on as one.

YOUR WISER BODY – YOUR PHYSICAL BEING

Have you ever stopped to think about your body? I mean really think about its significance? Your body is your home in this life. When it breaks or is destroyed, you don't get to move. This is the only "house" you get in this life so you must take care of it.

1. Eat a Healthy Diet. You read about new ways of eating almost daily. But in the end, it always comes down to the basics: lots of fresh fruits and vegetables (preferably organic), whole grains, light on the meat and fats and lots of water. We are truly what we eat, and it is clearly manifested as we age.

2. Exercise. Everyone searches for the fountain of youth…here it is. Combine exercise with a healthy diet, and your body will thank you for years to come. Which exercise program? That's up for debate. The most important thing is to find something you enjoy and can engage in daily.

3. Quit Smoking. This decision affects every part of your body. Your bones will be stronger, your heart will be happier; your blood pressure will decrease, your brain will receive more oxygen, and you will have fewer wrinkles. Your entire body, your family and friends, your pets and the Earth will thank you.

YOUR WISER BEING – YOUR SPIRIT

Are you tired of being told to act your age or that you are too old for "that"? Perhaps your life lacks focus? These action steps will help bring you back…to you!

1. Start a Gratitude Journal. The entries remind you of all the good in your life and make you feel better when you are down.

Writing gratitudes also encourages you to keep positive thoughts in mind.

2. Laugh. It strengthens your immune system, improves cardio-vascular function, releases all sorts of good chemicals into the body, improves thinking, and diminishes physical and emotional pain. As a bonus, it just may confuse others around you.

3. Play. Let the inner child in you come out. As "grown ups" it is easy to get bogged down in seriousness and responsibilities. Build sand castles, skip rope, play water balloons or make mud pies with your best friend as ways to stimulate the child within.

YOUR WISER LIFE – THE BUSINESS OF YOU

Having a successful aging experience includes having the resources and protection required to support your chosen lifestyle. It's never too early or too late to start building the life you want.

1. Invest in Yourself First. Allocate a certain dollar amount or percentage to put aside for every dollar you receive. It's up to you to decide on the amount that works best for your overall financial balance. Touch it only when you are ready to invest.

2. Retirement Accounts. Contribute the maximum allowed to your retirement account regularly. Educate yourself about your investment choices and get assistance with retirement planning. Start now.

3. Protection. Learn about long-term care insurance, asset protection, trusts, wills and the like. You will want your hard-earned money to stay with you and your designated heirs.

YOUR WISER COMMUNITY—BEING PART OF THE WHOLE

1. Donate Life. Become a blood, organ, or bone marrow donor. Until science figures out how to grow body tissue and body parts, it's up to each of us to donate our blood, bone marrow, eyes, skin and organs, so that others may be helped when we are ready to move on. What a grand feeling!

2. Practice Giving. Practice "random acts of kindness" and "give it forward" daily. Some examples are paying the toll for the driver behind you, holding the door open for others, picking up litter just because it is there, and taking someone's cart back to the grocery store. Regardless of your belief in "karma," doing good just plain feels good.

3. Reach Out to Others. Human beings are social creatures. It's a good reminder that you and the people around you are not alone. Recent studies have cited evidence that older adults do better when they are not isolated. As individuals, we thrive in various degrees of community. It's imperative that as we age we continue to develop our communities and networks.

YOUR WISER MIND—THE INSIDE OF YOU

This is really where you can make a difference. Everything starts here and stops here. Trying to get healthy? It will be impossible if your mind says otherwise.

1. Learn Something New. Learn something that you've always wanted to learn. It could be painting, pottery, papermaking, flying, a language, or an instrument. Learning something stimulates your brain and brings you joy. The return on investment is priceless!

2. Protect Your Brain. What is healthy for the body is healthy for the brain. This includes a diet low in fat and high in fruits, vegetables, and whole grains. Avoid chemicals harmful to your brain such as smoking, alcohol, and drugs.

3. Include Antioxidants in Your Diet and Supplements. These include vitamins C, E, beta-carotene, and selenium. Antioxidants slow the breakdown and aging of body cells, including brain cells.

THE OLDERWISERWOMAN – BRINGING IT ALL TOGETHER

It all comes down to this one concept. Aging is an inside job, and we need to adjust our "aging attitude" in order to age successfully. Look around you. Why is your 94-year-old neighbor younger than the 39 year old in the next block? What do you see yourself doing at 94? It's time to grow into yourself...the woman you are meant to be.

None of this works without the proper attitude. We are what we think. So think about and act on living a healthy and vibrant life. That's what Successful Aging is all about!

BARBARA C. PHILLIPS, NP is a board certified Geriatric and Family Nurse Practitioner with more than a few decades of experience. Her patients (the majority of them being older women) began asking intriguing questions about aging and the shared experiences of women. This led to the establishment of OlderWiserWomen™ where women are inspired to the freedom, magic, and wisdom of successful aging. Visit www.OlderWiserWomen.com for your copy of "Celebrating You: 50 Tips for Vibrant Living."

⌒

CHAPTER 11

Reprogramming Our Bodies for Optimum Wellness

EMMA SHARP, LAC., MS

TODAY GOOD HEALTH IS NO LONGER CONSIDERED MERELY THE ABSENCE OF DISEASE; it is the ability to achieve and maintain a state of physical and psychological well-being. This means not only experiencing peak physical functioning, but also having balanced emotions, behavior and communication with others.

While there are numerous healing practices to help achieve radiant health, I'll be sharing some insights about one of the most cutting-edge therapies available today: Nutripuncture. This modality enables your body to realize its optimal state of wellness.

Nutripuncture is endocellular nutrition that works on the energy system of the body (organs and meridians) in a similar way to acupuncture. It is in a chewable pill form however, widening the benefits of acupuncture to the large number of people who are frightened of needles.

Nutripuncture consists of different combinations of trace minerals that transfer specific electromagnetic information to the cells of the body, rather like programming a computer. Every cell in the body has a unique program and function. For example, a healthy breast cell "looks" and behaves in a certain way, which is very different from how a healthy thyroid cell "looks" and behaves. Disease originates from cells replicating and functioning in abnormal ways.

Each cell not only has a physical identity, but also a behavioral, emotional and communication aspect, which reflects a person's experience in life. Influences such as life events, inherited tendencies, family upbringing and environmental factors can cause physical and emotional trauma that disturb the functioning of the organs and meridians, and therefore, the cells. Nutripuncture can be used to break the cycle of disturbance and poor cellular programming by energetically reprogramming the cells, thus allowing the body to achieve a better state of health—physically and emotionally. Restoring the body's meridians is also a powerful tool in the prevention of disease.

FIRST STEPS

The first step in working with Nutripuncture is to take Yin/Yang, which is a general cellular nutrition regulator for the energy of the body. If a body is "yin yang positive," which can be determined by taking the pulse, then most of the energy in the body is flowing in the appropriate way, and chronic disease is less likely to develop. Conversely, disease manifests more easily when the body is "yin yang negative" and the energy is not flowing in the best way. There are a series of thirty-eight nutrients, which can be used with Yin/Yang to address specific physical or emotional symptoms.

An important part of working with Nutripuncture is ensuring that the body is in harmony with the passage of the seasons. Different times of the year stimulate the body in different ways, and each season has an action on specific organs and meridians, which makes them more sensitive. Certain emotional and physical symptoms are more likely to manifest at particular times of the year, and by nourishing the relevant vital currents (meridians), Nutripuncture can help prevent these seasonal symptoms, enabling the body to be more in harmony with its environment. During each season, there is also a sense (taste, hearing, smell, sight and touch) that is the most active.

ACHIEVING HEALTH THROUGH EVERY SEASON

Spring is a time of creativity, bursting through the buds of the season. The key meridians and organs that are active at this time are the liver and the gallbladder. The emotions that correspond to these organs are anger and resentment. The antidote to these emotions is forgiveness, so this time is a good time to wipe the grudge slate clean. Physically, digestion can be impaired, especially of fats, and energy can be depleted. The sense associated with springtime is touch, so issues could arise related to this sense. Nourish this time of year with Nutripuncture: Yin/Yang plus #11 and #30.

The meridian and organ pair related to summer is the heart and small intestine. The heart represents the ability to love self and others, and the small intestine is related to making good choices. Capitalizing on the creativity initiated by the spring, the summer is the time to envision projects. The sense of the season is sight, which relates to not only the physical sense, but also the ability to perceive one's heart's desire. There can be a tendency to gain weight, become depressed or want to drink more alcohol at this time. Cardiac pathologies or problems with assimilation can be particularly emphasized (Yin/Yang plus #04 and 13).

With the season of late summer, the stomach and pancreas become active. There may be digestive or blood sugar issues, and the sense related to this season is taste. The stomach represents action and the pancreas follow-through. The projects initiated in summer are now in full swing (Yin/Yang plus #10 and #18).

The fall is the season of the lungs and the colon. Now is the time to harvest the rewards of one's efforts. What inspiration can be derived from one's achievements? The ability to feel inspired comes from a healthy sense of smell, which is more sensitive in the fall. Lung problems and autoimmune disease such as chronic fatigue may manifest at this time as well as issues with constipation or colitis. Self-confidence is the emotional hallmark of the lungs, with the colon enabling us to be organized (Yin/Yang plus #20 and #05).

As the nights of winter draw in, we turn inward and reflect on what we have "harvested" in our lives. This is a time of introspection, before the seasonal cycle starts again with the dawn of spring. The kidney and bladder meridians are the most active at this time. The kidney corresponds to fear, and the bladder is related to our ability to reflect and see ourselves clearly. How are we listening to others and ourselves? Hearing is the sense related to winter. Emotionally, anxiety or lack of clarity may be present at this time. Physically, problems with the kidneys, bladder or back may manifest (Yin/yang #22 and #31).

RELEASING TRAUMA

In addition to using Yin/Yang plus combinations of the thirty-eight nutrients to address physical or emotional symptoms during each season, Nutripuncture can also be used sequentially. Sequences are a series of five nutrients taken in a prescribed order that target a particular organ, meridian, gland or part of the body, providing it with more precise instructions for optimal functioning. For example, sequences can be as specific as working on a specific joint or bone. A certified practitioner must prescribe this stage of Nutripuncture therapy.

Sequences can also be used to relieve the effects of traumatic experiences. Events such as car accidents, abortion, rape, divorce, death and incest all cause disturbances to the meridians, which can be restored using the nutrients. Nutripuncture cannot change the fact that an event happened, but it can energetically restore the body so that a person can recover and move past the event to live a healthy and more balanced life. For example, many times a rape victim is unable to enjoy sexual relations following the trauma. By restoring the meridians that were disturbed as a result of the rape, this person can develop the ability to once again have a healthy intimate relationship. Nutripuncture can also enable a person to forgive more easily by restoring the meridians disturbed by the grievance. Sequences need only be taken between four and six weeks.

Today, health is becoming more about the total human experience. It is not about simply fixing physical or emotional symptoms, but it is connected with investigating why these symptoms have manifested. We are the sum total of our experience, as well as the experience of our parents and ancestors. If we really want to lay claim to our present and improve the future for our children, then we will need to release the negative patterning that no longer serves us. Reprogramming the cells using Nutripuncture provides us with a means of achieving this optimal state of wellness.

EMMA SHARP is an acupuncturist practicing in Santa Monica. She treats patients with chronic illness, those in pain, wanting to lose weight, stop smoking or just stay healthy. She also uses herbs, homeopathics, nutritional counseling and supplementation, flower remedies and aromatherapy. Emma's unique offering is Nutripuncture. She is the first acupuncturist in the States to be certified in this modality. For more information contact www.emmasharp.com or call (310) 829-6829. Phone sessions are available for patients from outside the area.

CHAPTER 12

Walking in Confidence

RAQUEL SMITH

EVERYONE WANTS TO BE TOTALLY CONFIDENT. Faith of a mustard seed can move a mighty mountain. However, without the confidence in oneself to know that it can really happen, it will not happen. It does not take a decade to develop confidence. It just takes a simple decision. Once you take one step at a time, you can develop total confidence. No matter where you are from, who you are, or your personality, you can develop confidence to succeed.

Imagine for a moment, a little girl growing up in the ghetto in a third world country in a single parent home of three children and a mother. All she saw around her was total poverty and lack. There was no confidence or hope of a brighter future. However, she excelled in school and developed a deep relationship with God. Somehow, through her love of reading and taking part in all the extracurricular activities at school, she found out that there was a vast world outside of her living environment. A different world; one she longed for.

She learned to internalize her true emotions and appeared tough on the outside. To others, she seemed to be a strong, confident girl.

However, she saw it as a way of surviving her environment. She had to put on a tough face to avoid any confrontations. She carried that persona through to her adult life.

I was that girl. I generally tell people that I spent the first thirty years of my life sleep walking. I was living, but I was not in total awareness. A series of events happened in my life that slowly opened my eyes. The day I woke up and started living fully aware, my world opened up and I have been walking down the road of success ever since.

I moved from a state of total darkness to a state of complete expanded awareness. I have grown into a totally confident woman. Confidence is not a destination, it is a journey. As the title suggests, you walk in confidence daily. It is a practice that becomes a part of your subconscious so much so that you do things that you would be afraid of doing without even thinking about it. Confidence is feeling the fear and doing it anyway. Confidence will propel you to success in any circumstance. Total confidence wipes out every ounce of fear. Once you exude total confidence, success is inevitable. You will realize that you have all the resources you need to succeed. People will be drawn to you because of your total confidence. People will want to talk to you, not even knowing why because there is something like a magnet attracting them to you. This is what total confidence does for you.

Here are seven steps to propel you to total confidence:

1. ACKNOWLEDGE THAT YOU ARE A GREAT PERSON

Most of us were taught not to think too highly of ourselves as a child growing up. Even as an adult, others may think that we are too cocky if we believe too much in ourselves. Well, I say forget about all of those teachings and be proud of who you are. You must appreciate and love yourself in order to be totally confident.

2. CHANGE YOUR THINKING

Thoughts create reality. Your personal powers are a direct result of the way you think. The way you think is a choice. Stop thinking negatively. Negative thoughts were learned through our environment and the way we were raised. Therefore, positive thoughts can be learned through reading and listening to motivational self-development books. When negative thoughts or images pop up in your head you can quickly change them to something positive. Over time, it will become unconscious and you will become a totally positive person.

3. LEARN TO BE MORE INTUITIVE

There is a voice inside of us that always tells us the right way to go, if we will only listen. Some people may say it is the Holy Spirit; some may say it is their North Star, sixth sense or intuition. I have found that whenever I don't listen to it and do the opposite, I always do the wrong thing, without fail. Before you make any decision, take a moment and listen to your inner voice; it will never steer you wrong.

4. TAKE RISKS

Look at new experiences as opportunities to learn and grow as opposed to occasions to win or lose. By doing so, you will be open to new possibilities and an increase in self-acceptance. Doing otherwise turns every experience into an opportunity for failure and thus stifles your growth and confidence.

5. CHANGE YOUR SELF-TALK

Too often our daily self-talk includes phrases of failure, self-doubt and fear. Use your self-talk as an opportunity to counter harmful assumptions. We tend to tell ourselves that we are going to fail before we even start. Turn that around; choose positive things to say. Tell yourself you will be a success and that you will achieve your goal no matter what others say.

6. SELF-EVALUATION

Learn to evaluate yourself outside of what others think. It is only natural for us to want the acceptance of others and feel successful if other people think that we are successful. We get caught up in internal turmoil because we constantly rely on the opinions of others. Focusing internally on how you feel about yourself and your achievements will give you a stronger sense of self and empowerment. This will prevent you from giving your power away to someone else.

7. DAILY POSITIVE ACTIONS

Always begin and end the day with a prayer and meditation. This practice gets you ready to face the world and at the end of the day gets your mind relaxed. Say positive affirmations that propel you to success. Always write at least three successes that you accomplished each day in a journal just for that purpose. Whenever you feel discouraged, read your success journal to remind yourself that you are already a confident, successful person. Surround yourself with positive people. You become who you associate with the most.

I guarantee if you practice each and every one of these steps consistently, you will develop into a totally confident person on your way to massive success. It will not happen overnight; however, once you make the decision to move forward there is no turning back. All of the seven steps must be practiced in order to achieve your goal of becoming totally confident. As I stated earlier in the chapter, confidence is a journey; therefore, these steps are things you must practice every day until they become totally unconscious.

This may sound cliché, but if I can turn my life around and become so confident that others notice there is a difference in me, you can do it too. Walking in confidence means that you are allowing yourself to be open to new experiences and opportunities for success. Total confidence allows you to do things you would not normally do in your previous state. Total confidence will allow you to walk away from a lousy relationship and an unfulfilling job. These are some of the actions that you were once afraid to take because you lacked the confidence to make the move. Total confidence will allow you to feel free and self-assured to get whatever your heart desires and more.

Above all things, keep in mind that you have all the resources you need inside of you to succeed. Go forth and walk in confidence!

RAQUEL SMITH is a Certified Master Results Coach, and she is certified in hypnosis and Creation Technologies©. Raquel specializes in relationship values alignment, which builds strong bonds in couples and families. Raquel has extensive experience in people relation and coaching to success. Raquel's company, Golden Life Coaching does one-on-one, couples, family, and group sessions. The company also does seminars. You may contact (866) 394-3081 or email info@golden-lifecoaching.com for more information. To subscribe to the monthly newsletter go to www.goldenlifecoaching.com.

CHAPTER 13

Finding Your Own Voice

LYNNE VELLING

AT MY ORDINATION CEREMONY IN 1998, I declared that my ministry would be communication, and that I would write a book entitled "Finding Your Own Voice," the same as my ministerial thesis. I didn't know at the time how these statements of intention would manifest. The first intention unfolded with my creating my own business, Velling & Associates Communication Training; the second is beginning with this chapter. There is nothing quite like "putting it out there" to kick start manifestation.

Everyone has a Voice. Voice is Sound; Voice is Presence; Voice is Pride; Voice is Power—Voice is all this. Finding your Voice once doesn't end the process; you will likely need to find it again, and again—as you grow and evolve with your life's adventures. It's a shared experience, a necessary experience for most of us.

Have you seen the movie "Little Voice"? It's about a young woman's search to find her own voice, rather than being shut up by the overriding words of an egocentric mother or using the voices of movie stars she emulates by lip-syncing. Are you looking for the same...feeling you have little, or no Voice? Pulitzer Prize winner,

Tony Award nominee and Presidential Inaugural poet Maya Angelou refused to speak for four years to anyone but her brother after a traumatic sexual assault when she was eight. All the while, she listened—within and without, to all the voices her soul expressed and to others around her. Her distillation of emotion birthed a Voice that, to this day, has profound impact—both in words and in the depth of her Presence.

The self-discovery in finding your own Voice takes courage and risk. We make mistakes, we stumble, and we suffer embarrassment to grow our "courage" muscle. The more we practice, the stronger we get, the same as we do with our physical bodies.

Voice is an ever-evolving sound of head-heart-gut. It's about reaching in and discovering who's there and sharing what's important to you. Verbalizing—giving voice to words—empowers your life experience; it affirms your Presence, your aliveness and your validity in the world.

When you affirm your Presence, you express your power—your "say." This occurs with the sounds you choose to use, speaking with words that do not diminish yourself, and carrying a sense of awareness of yourself and others. Being aware is key—it's listening with a "third ear," as founder of Speaking Circles International®, Lee Glickstein, says. We need to hear *how* we are so we know *who* we are—then we can consciously change what we perceive.

The key question is: Do you *want* to find your own Voice? If so, being aware of the need is the challenge. Taking on the search or journey is the commitment. If not, ask yourself, what Voice are you using, if not your own? How does THAT feel? I feel it's like not being in your own skin.

Some choose words to express: poetry, prose writing, song writing. Some find their Voice in creative endeavors: dancing, painting, designing, sculpting, developing math puzzles. Many others find their Voice in the every day: cutting trees, cleaning houses, arranging food. You create value when you have Voice. No Voice is less valuable. As in the chain of life, everything matters. Every Voice expressed is a person who feels the experience of Life.

The harder you push yourself to hear your Voice, the more stress you experience. If you can find your Voice by letting yourself explore, more than likely you will find it, OR it will find you. "Getting unstuck is not so much about effort, I realized—it's more about moving forward with the natural flow of things. Power requires cooperation," says actress Anna Deveare Smith.

Cooperation occurs with mind, body, emotion and spirit working together to let you see how and who you are in the world. We get stuck in expression through fear. That's it. That's what holds us back. That's really the poison of self-defeating talk and action. Cooperation is willingness.

HOW DID I BECOME AWARE AND HOW CAN YOU?

My Voice changes occurred most dramatically through defining moments that "shocked" me into keener awareness. I was already aware of myself at various times, but the joke of awareness is that sometimes we take it for granted and become lazy, saying "I am aware," like saying "I am Christian," but not practicing it. It is in the practicing of consciousness while letting yourself go about your ordinary business that you discover the unique nature of who you are—your Presence. "Consciousness makes me conscious," says world-renowned healer Rev. Rosalyn Bruyere. Presence is felt, once you've discovered it, even when you are silent. Your silence speaks. Notice. It's true.

Having a Voice means letting out who you are so people can experience you, recognize you, support you; and allowing yourself success in the eyes of others. It may mean changing your voice as your personality changes, so your Voice resonates your power and Presence more effectively. It has been said, "Change your Voice, change your Life."

He just had to say it in "penguin"... After striking out with stories he wanted to tell, Jordan Roberts finds his voice in translation.
—MARY MCNAMARA, *Los Angeles Times,* AUGUST 2005

As you discover many voices within, know that they all emanate from one. That one is You. You can choose a specific voice, one of many you hear inside, to share your Voice. Voice is a reflection of your soul; it's a life-long adventure in being and becoming. In finding your own Voice, you clarify your Presence.

Even First Ladies of this country have needed to change their Voice to become powerful role models of awareness and courage.

"Laura Bush raises her voice (a bit)"
(in regard to helping her husband, George W. Bush, with his 2004 presidential campaign)
—JUDY KEEN AND RICHARD BENEDETTO,
USA Today, June 2004

"Her Home Silent, Nancy Reagan Found a Voice on Alzheimer's Research"
—BERNARD WEINTRAUB AND ELIZABETH BUMILLER,
The New York Times, June 2004

IMPACT OF A SPEAKER

Are you aware, per surveys and analysis, that ...

Verbal impact	—YOUR WORDS	— is 7%
Vocal impact	—YOUR TONE, RANGE, APPEAL, CREDIBILITY	— is 38%
Visual impact	—YOUR STANCE, EYE CONTACT, LOOKS, GESTURES	— is 55%

... of communication?

Your Presence, your silent Voice, is what listeners feel immediately, without even opening your mouth. When you do, you combine your silent Voice with the sound of voice and words to give resonance to and radiate your Presence.

WHAT TO DO

Focus on Process: Voice is the combination of all these elements:

— Mind: Organize, memorize, recognize, observe more closely those you admire

— Body: Breathe, exercise, build your energy, develop good posture

— Emotions: Feel, acknowledge fears, be authentic, laugh, get therapy if necessary

— Spirit: Synthesize in your heart, risk, challenge yourself, build awareness

Focus on Projection: Explore, expand, develop through:

— Chanting

— Singing

— Storytelling

— Vocalized prayer

- - -

—   Getting voice coaching

—   Taking voice classes

—   Taping yourself on audio and video

      - - -

—   Leading

—   Mentoring

I COULDN'T SAY IT BETTER

Say this prayer. It will help you find your Voice. Believe you can; it is there for you to know, embrace and love.

Creator, give me the courage to find my Voice, to make real. It is such a habit to hold silence, to feel the moment of manifestation arrive and to make no sound. We waste so many words, so much breath, so much time, on the petty and ultimately destructive. Remind me of the power I hold in my throat; may I not choke on it, or use it frivolously. Every sound is a vibration, and every vibration is felt everywhere in the universe. I ask you to help me to live as though I remembered that.
       —Rev. Susan Brown, 1996

I wish you courage in finding your own Voice on your life's journey.

RESOURCES:

Vellingcommtraining.com
SpeakingCircles.com
SpeakerServices.com
Toastmasters.org
DaleCarnegie.com
Be Heard Now!, Lee Glickstein
Feel the Fear and Do It Anyway, Susan Jeffers, Ph. D.
Unleash The Power Within, Anthony Robbins

LYNNE VELLING, principal of Velling & Associates Communication Training, has extensive experience as a speech coach/consultant, help-ing people find a powerful, effective voice. Lynne is also a certified facilitator for Speaking Circles International®, a creator/trainer of Customer Service programs and an ESL instructor. A 20+ year Distinguished Toastmaster, Lynne is a minister of the Healing Light Center Church. With communication as her ministry, she assists indi-viduals with personal empowerment: www.vellingcommtraining.com, (626) 614-0411.

CHAPTER 14

The Turning Point

ELAINE WILSON

"TODAY'S TRENDS IN FINE ARTS ARE UNACCEPTABLE TO ME," I kept repeating to myself for months. My heart ached at the thought of no longer supporting myself by creating art as I had done for over twenty-five years.

I stood at a turning point. Having been told by trusted friends that if I wanted to "get to a new destination," I needed to take the *First Step*. I asked them, what was the *First Step*? "Put into writing what you love. Follow your passion."

I sat down and discovered a love for living things, design, and the environment were at the top of my list. How could these be combined into a business? Become a garden/landscape designer! Design, the environment, and gardening have always been important parts of my life and expressions of joy. My focus would be to help heal the earth by using only organic methods of landscape design. The plant selections would be beautiful, utilizing low-water-usage plants that absorb toxins from both the air and soil. Creating beautiful low-maintenance landscapes would be another important component.

Now for **Action Step #1.** "Get a computer and learn how to use it." After buying the best computer system for my personal and business needs and taking three months to learn as much and as quickly as possible—the computer became the passport to my new career.

Action Step #2: "Sign up at a local university and take some classes. Become willing to do whatever it takes to reach the goal."

My knowledge of plants, gardening, and interest in preserving the environment was paying off. Learning more about my business continued as an "independent study" and a labor of love.

- Taking seminars is a valuable method of exposing oneself to the most recent business techniques and skills for the small business owner.

- On-line business courses are available with free workbooks and support.

- Video conferences have kept my mind open to new ideas. Teleconferences are also valuable.

Action Step #3: "You must network. Register your company name. You need a business card. You need to take some business seminars and get a business license."

- I joined two networking groups that a dear friend had recommended. Within two months of networking, I earned $7,000 from two projects. I was in business!

- **GardensByDesign with GardensToGo,** the registered name of my company, was suggested by another "networking sister."

- I designed and printed my own business cards. That first card changed as I learned that nothing is "set in stone," and it's expected that marketing tools evolve with experience.

- Fliers and brochures came next. I assembled the materials into "presentation packets" for prospective clients. This provided an effective, simple way to show the quality of my work. After all, a picture is worth a thousand words.

- Getting a business license was important to me. A business license made my company "real" in my mind. I also could work from home, knowing that I was complying with the laws of my city.

Action Step #4 gave me butterflies. "Speak your business in thirty seconds or less," I was told by a networking presenter. Speaking in public and to strangers about my business made me nervous. "Reps" had always made business contacts for me.

It was essential for me to practice speaking, with support from those who have successful businesses and lives. Finding mentors who know how to get beyond snags in the road was and is essential. Mentors who share creative ideas that would be missed had I depended solely on my internal dialogue.

- Taking "baby steps," sometimes for ten seconds at a time, taught me to keep information short and to the point. Paying someone to coach me and give me "tag lines" also helped tremendously.

- My first ten-minute talk terrified me. I did it anyway, and now I know that people will hear and remember what I share if they are engaged and not "talked at." Get listeners involved. Ask questions. Use humor. Use visual aids.

- My second project hit a snag when I had no idea what the client wanted. A promising client relationship became difficult. A wise mentor who had over twenty years in the real estate business gave me insight to new communication skills. I changed how I communicated with the client. Everything turned around, and I continue to do work for this client today.

"Get a website" was suggested as *Action Step #5.* As a novice, not only in the business world but also in cyberspace, I had no idea what to do or what to expect from a web designer.

- I hired a designer and ultimately substituted the original website for my bi-monthly newsletter that I created from scratch. How's that for a former "computer Illiterate"?

- Marketing is essential. Finding the right vehicle for my business is a continuing exercise. Having the courage to explore new marketing ideas that resonate is an exciting part of this journey. My creativity is a continuing asset.

- My *GardensByDesign* newsletter costs me no money to design and produce since I do it all myself. When my subscription list is over 1,000 and/or I have products to sell, then I will select one of the many support companies to manage my subscription list.

Listening to my creative inner voice is *Action Step # 6.* It's okay for me to disagree with another's point of view. There are a couple of "Big Time Speakers" who have stated from the speaker's platform that, "By the time people are sixty, they are either dead or dead-broke." How absurd in the 21st Century to utter or repeat this erroneous statistic. The "Baby Boomers" are among the most financially secure of all generations, and most are looking forward to new, challenging careers and/or public service. Denis Waitley says, "Most multi-millionaires are made after age 50."

Any pre-conceptions I have held about business and how to be successful have been dissolved by the wonderful people who continue to guide me. "Business is spiritual; having ethics is a cornerstone of success, and being my authentic self" continue to be stressed by many seminar leaders, business mentors and "knowing" friends.

In discovering amazing tools and new ways of approaching the world of business, I have found abilities and talents I had no idea I possessed. Most of my life, many false beliefs had kept me from realizing the benefits earned by my creativity. I believed that business was boring, and it would halt my creative juices. I had turned over the financial benefits of being a self-employed artist to galleries and art reps in the past. Now, I was realizing 100 percent of my business profits.

When I began this business adventure, I consciously let go of my career in Fine Art. Now, wonder of wonders, "My Life as a Spiral" has me growing upward and looking forward to eventually turning the garden/landscape side of my company over to a young person, while keeping the right to my company name.

The company's new division will be "Sculpture for the Garden," which will be my focus. My life today is as exciting and creative as it was when I first began as a professional artist. "What is truly yours will return to you."

ELAINE WILSON is the proud owner of GardensByDesign with GardensToGo located in Southern California. Planting selection is based on beauty, low-water-usage, and maximum absorption of toxins from the air and soil. Organic methods only are used (no pesticides ever applied). GardensToGo designs and installs organic, portable container gardens for decks, patios, and terraces that move when you move. Learn more about organic landscaping: Sign up for GardensByDesign, FREE Newsletter. E-mail: elaine1111@earthlink.net Phone: (310) 320- 4789.

PART II

BUSINESS AND
FINANCIAL FULFILLMENT

⌒

CHAPTER 15

Is Your Heart at Work?

AVGHI CONSTANTINIDES, MA

ASK YOURSELF THESE QUESTIONS:

- *Do you leap out of bed looking forward to the day ahead?*
- *Do you feel excited about going to work?*
- *When you walk into your place of work do you smile?*

I OFTEN COME ACROSS PEOPLE WHO ARE UNHAPPY in their jobs. Some are stuck there, and some are in transition, waiting for their next opportunity. Either way, their unhappiness leads to imbalance in their entire system, mentally, emotionally and yes, physically. I call this energy your vital force. One way of leaking this energy/vital force is through criticizing, complaining and blaming others. If changing jobs is not an option at this moment, you might consider an alternate option, a change in attitude.

So if you find yourself in a job that does not fulfill you, listen to yourself when you are around your friends and co-workers. Are you criticizing, complaining and blaming? When you catch yourself doing this, realize that you are leaking precious energy from your vital force and it is time to change your focus. Pour your energy into actions that either move you to a different job or change your *attitude*.

WHAT DOES THE SITUATION REQUIRE?

If you can't stand your work place, honor that and move on.
Action always clears deadlocked energy.
Be *honest* with yourself and listen to your *heart*. When you truly feel good about something you will give it your all. Be true to the situation, event, or circumstance you're facing.

IS MOVING TO ANOTHER JOB GOING TO SOLVE YOUR PROBLEM?

You still have to take yourself along.
Make peace with yourself first. Is it really the job that is the problem or is it *you?* Stop resisting it and use your energy to express gratefulness for the job.
Change your attitude and turn the hate energy into gratitude energy. Focus inward and deal with the negative energies that you dislike in yourself. When you are truly ready, you will find it easy to move into work situation that you love. Sometimes we can be in a place we don't like, but cannot move on until we are ready to change.

IT'S TIME FOR A CHANGE!

When you were a teenager maybe you listened to your parent's goals instead of your own. Go back to school and learn what you really wanted to do in the first place. Now you can listen to your *heart* and follow your true *passion*.

WHAT IS YOUR PASSION?

Think about a five year old child who's been asked what they want to do when they grow up. They may give you ten answers; they don't think from their heads but from their hearts.

Think, what you would really love to do for work, what is your *passion*?

Be the five year old and just let it out! Be creative, its playtime, give yourself at least ten minutes to do this.

FULFILLING YOUR HEART'S PASSION

So now you have an idea, a dream, a goal.

1. What are the steps needed to take you there? (classes, networking, new resume)

2. Write a personal business plan. This is a road map. It does not have to be perfect, so be creative with it. (you can even email me, and I will give you an outline for this)

HOW TO TURN YOUR WORK LIFE INTO YOUR LIFE'S WORK

You may be a lawyer whose work leaves you unfulfilled so you become a part time volunteer and donate some of your services to a cause that has meaning for you. Maybe the big money comes from clients who you may not always wish to be associated with, but then your next project could be living one of your dreams.

A patient of mine has a debilitating disease; she had been trying to use her creativity by making jewelry, flower arrangements and handbags, but nothing really seemed to hold her interest. From the recent loss of her beloved dog, she started a business making memory bracelets for pet owners and found healing in the creativeness. She has so much drive and is so excited. She donates a percentage of her profits to an animal rescue group. It's the first time in a long time that I have seen a spark in her eyes. She has found her enthusiasm and love in her work.

SHIFT YOUR THINKING

Maybe you are just gloomy in your life, and it's not your work. What can you do to change this? Are you still stuck in your childhood or holding onto ugly old stuff? You can move forward.

I have always loved my work.

I started out working in London at a five-star-hotel. The staff was so much fun to be around that I loved going to work. When I lived in Africa, I worked at another hotel. I lived in the jungle, and every free moment I was out exploring and on safari. It was the most amazing time of my life.

When I came to the United States I worked with children and learned enormously from them. I love working with children. I also worked in the supplement industry; it was fun helping people with alternatives to western medicine. Looking back on it, I've realized that all of my jobs served to help people and I love that!

Eventually my passion led me to healing people through homeopathy. I have been in practice since 1995, and I always smile when I walk into my office. Five years ago I decided to be in a work place that supported my patients and my views on health. I opened up an alternative healing center to optimize people's health through different modalities, offer free education to the community and free healthcare to the underprivileged. This took five years to plan, and I held monthly meetings at my house, sharing my vision with people in the healing community.

While this was taking place, another opportunity dropped into my lap—the opportunity to teach others the practice of homeopathy.

I co-founded the Los Angeles School of Homeopathy where I am now the director.

TAKING CARE OF SELF

– *What are your hobbies?*
– *Are you fulfilling yourself outside of work?*
– *Do you replenish and relax outside of work?*

It is important to have your down time, to relax, switch off and just treat yourself gently. It could be a hike, a bubble bath, having a massage. One of my off switches is sailing, where all thoughts of things on land just start to melt away. It's my time away, my retreat, and my therapy. What is yours?

A friend recently had heart surgery, and we nearly lost him. Some months later his sister found him to be quite miserable and she asked him, "You have a second chance in life. Why are you so miserable?" Her comments made him think. He remembered how he was before and decided to make a shift. So he did change his tune and is now singing a much happier one.

You have millions of breaths each day and millions of chances to choose what you wish for in your life. Don't waste your precious time. *Honor* your *life*—it is worth it! Do what is your heart's desire and seek the work you really wish to do. I wish you success and happiness.

Sometimes people get a second chance at life. I always notice them because they stand out. They always have a smile on their face; they feel blessed and honored to be here another day. I wish I could gather up their energy and share it with others, but this energy has to come from within, and no one can give it to you.

Instead of working for a living, start loving the work you live for.

Find your passion and love the work that you do!

I wish you well on this path, and if I can support you in any way, please don't hesitate to contact me.

⌒

AVGHI CONSTANTINIDES, D.hom HMC MA, has been named one of the best homeopaths California has to offer. She holds a BS in nutrition, a diploma in homeopathy, a Masters in homeopathy and is a Homeopathic Master Clinician. She is the Director and Co-founder of the Los Angeles School of Homeopathy, Director of Centre for Life, alternative healing center and has been in practice since 1995. Reach her at: 310 279-5010 www.homeopathyforlife.com www.lahomeopathicschool.com or www.lacentreforlife.com.

⌒

CHAPTER 16

Breaking Through the Real Glass Ceiling:

Raising Our Consciousness

PHYLISS FRANCIS, MA, CLC

Whether you think you're a loser or think you're a winner,
you're right. —HENRY FORD

WHEN WE HEAR THE TERM "GLASS CEILING" what image comes to
our minds? Most people immediately imagine a barrier that women
and people of color confront that prevents them from moving up
the corporate ladder. The "glass ceiling" was a term coined after
the civil rights era when women and ethnic minorities continued to
bump up against a transparent limitation. They were unable to
move past a certain point to the next level professionally even
though they could see others achieve higher levels. Whether or
not you have experienced the "glass ceiling" in the traditional
sense, you may have had an encounter that left you feeling held
back due to something you perceived in your physical environment.

So how do we move beyond this barrier or glass ceiling in our
professional and personal lives? Instead of focusing on the external
limitations in our lives, I would like to examine the levels of

consciousness that we are resisting within ourselves. I will take you beyond the corporate concept of the "glass ceiling" to the "real glass ceiling of consciousness," or awareness, within yourself.

If you knew you could not fail, what would you do? Think about this for a minute. Would you be a writer, a pilot, doctor or lawyer? Or would you be an artist, a teacher or entrepreneur? Whatever you desire, allow yourself to step into the possibility of what it would be and dream. Go ahead and play for a moment...

Now that you have that goal or vision in mind, please answer these questions. Why haven't you done it? What's stopping you? Your answers might be: *I do not have enough time, money, or resources.* Or, *I am not qualified because of my education, gender or race?* In other words, what is your "glass ceiling"?

Take a moment to acknowledge your glass ceiling whatever it might be. You might say: *Check my bank account! Look at my schedule! Look at the statistics involving socio-economics, race and gender!* But before we take a look at your physical environment, let's check out what is living in your consciousness and start there. If your outer reality is a reflection of your inner reality, then we must start with your consciousness.

Before you can break through the barriers that you perceive, you must first break through the barriers that are present in your own consciousness. For example, my client Linda* hired me to assist her with manifesting a new job. During our first session, Linda complained continually that her work hours were too long and included weekends, her income was low, and she was not inspired. When I attempted to focus Linda on the elements she desired in an ideal job, she would revert back to the external obstacles working against her: *I am too old! There are no good jobs available! I do not have enough education, experience or training!* These statements reflected her *real* "glass ceiling." Once Linda realized these perceived limitations were reflections of her consciousness and not

*All names have been changed.

her direct physical experience, she was able to refocus. Within two weeks, Linda was hired for a more flexible, higher paying, new job that suddenly became available within her company.

Like Linda, I believe you can begin to make a shift in your consciousness and break through the *real* glass ceiling if you follow the five key strategies below.

1. UTILIZE THE TECHNIQUES OF CONSCIOUS VISUALIZATION

Conscious Visualization allows you to create clarity about the goal or vision you would like to achieve and then picture your success as if it is already happening in your mind's eye.

For example, I worked with Lisa, an interior designer whose goal was to expand her business from remodeling small kitchens and bathrooms to designing multi-million dollar homes. She visualized herself attracting bigger jobs, but we also brought more depth to the visualization by including "feeling tones," which are the vivid, emotional responses and feelings associated with successfully living your ideal scene out as if it were available now. Through this daily practice of visualizing her ideal career, infused with the feeling tones of confidence and creativity, she retrained her consciousness to believe that she was worthy and deserving of attracting high-end contracts. Within two months Lisa manifested two redesigning contracts, a major hotel in the Caribbean, and a multi-million dollar home. She broke through her "glass ceiling" of consciousness that she was not worthy enough to attract her dream clients.

2. REMEMBER WHAT YOU FOCUS ON EXPANDS

Understand the universal principle, "What you focus on expands." If I told you today that I want to buy a blue Jaguar, why do we begin seeing blue Jaguars all over the place? Although the Jaguar Corporation did not unleash a warehouse full of blue

Jaguars for me because I declared it, I did choose to direct my intention on what it is I want. Consequently, my mind centers on whatever perpetuates my intention. This universal principle applies to our everyday lives whether we chose to focus on what is working in our life or what is not. Move your focus to the many possibilities awaiting you on the other side of the glass ceiling as opposed to the glass ceiling itself. Center your attention on what is working in your life so that you may notice the many positive opportunities appearing on your path.

3. TAKE AN ACTION STEP EVERY DAY

How do you eat an elephant? One bite at a time. Create a plan and take an action step every day towards your goal or vision, whether big or small. Action steps can be internal, which include aligning your consciousness with your goal through affirmations or conscious visualization. External action steps can include making a phone call or going to a meeting. Try not to focus on the enormity of the project, so break it down into bite-size pieces. I once worked with Deborah whose goal was to complete her first book, but the thought of writing the book overwhelmed her to the point where she could not take any action. We created a plan to write one page a day. Within eleven months, Deborah's book was finished! When taking an action step every day, do not forget to incorporate a support system that will hold you accountable like teaming up with a buddy, finding a mentor or hiring a life coach.

4. SURROUND YOURSELF WITH PEOPLE WHO EMPOWER YOUR VISION

Since *"birds of a feather flock together,"* it is important to fly with people who are moving towards your vision. Surround yourself with like-minded people who not only see your goal, or vision, but feel it. Nothing is more empowering than having people support your dream. Learn from your support group because there is no reason why you need to reinvent the wheel and start your journey from the ground up, especially when there are many others who already have paved the way.

5. BE PATIENT WITH THE PROCESS

Since our outer reality is a reflection of our inner reality, we must remember that it takes time to shift our consciousness. Your current consciousness is a habit that has been formed over years of experience so take time to cultivate the necessary shifts to be reflected in your professional and personal environments. Practice creates habits, so create successful habits. If you want the mountain to move, know that it takes time to move the mountain, so be patient with the process.

Although there are many strategies you can utilize to break through the *real* glass ceiling, only you have the power to follow them. Remember, if your outer reality is a reflection of your inner reality, then you have the ability to remove "the real glass ceiling" of your consciousness.

PHYLISS FRANCIS, MA, CLC is an insightful and empowering Certified Life Coach and facilitator. Through her company, Stop Talk Coaching (www.stoptalk.net), she coaches people to Live Life Out Loud! Phyliss has extensive experience and training in coaching, counseling, personal growth, self-development, transformation and spirituality. She holds a MA in Spiritual Psychology from the University of Santa Monica and a membership to the International Coaching Federation. Contact Phyliss for a complimentary coaching session: phyliss@stoptalk.net (310) 995-3101.

⌒

CHAPTER 17

Let's Play To Win!

RHONDA JOHNSON

ISN'T IT FUN PLAYING GAMES WITH CHILDREN? It's challenging to teach them unique strategies that encourage them to use the rules to their advantage. Games are fun for the young at heart as well, so from this moment...let's play the tax game, "It's What You KEEP That Counts!" And...let's play to win!

FACT: Your Biggest Single Expenditure is TAXES...35% or much more!

Every tax dollar you save drops to your bottom line. Simply put, you get to keep a dollar for every tax dollar you save.

STRATEGY: Learn How To Keep More of What You Make!

FACT: In this game, what you don't know can really hurt you.

Let's begin the game with the first question: "Do you work from home?"

The great news is that a business from home qualifies you for many deductions that cannot be achieved any other way.

When you establish your business from home, you are able to convert a portion of your existing non-deductible expenses to fully deductible business expenses. You are able to apply the PERCENTAGE of space used for the business.

As an example, let's say it's 13 percent of your home. Therefore 13 percent of your expenses such as your homeowners insurance, property insurance, mortgage interest and even the utilities become deductible.

A percentage deduction would also apply to maintenance costs, cleaning service, gardener, painting and remodeling of your business area. This 13 percent can be a big number. In addition, up to $100,000+ for purchase of equipment for the business may also be deducted.

STRATEGY: Have a product-based business and dramatically increase your Business Use Percentage (BUP)...

FACT: Beware of Myths...like having to show a profit three out of five years.

Wait just a minute. That's the Hobby Loss Rule. This misstatement of the actual law has been repeated so many times that it has risen to the status of an urban legend. Even my CPA husband thinks it's true. Amazon.com wrote off millions and millions of losses for over ten years. The reason they could do it was because they had the intent to produce a profit. Why would you start a business without having a profit motive? Even if you are unable to show a profit for a numbers of years, proving you are operating a legitimate business can be established just by having good business procedures. Operate like a business. Keep good records, advertise, develop your business knowledge and skills, spend an appropriate amount of time and have a written business plan. If your business is a pleasurable activity, the IRS could look for proof that your intent to make a profit is actively being pursued.

Why would any intelligent businessperson continue the same business for five years and not make a profit?

STRATEGY: Have a Clearly Defined and Documented Profit Motive.

FACT: Use the KISS Method for Your Record Keeping.

Keep **I**t **S**imple **S**tupid certainly applies to the dreaded documentation required when you have a business. Don't think complex; think simple. These are my suggested minimal steps you need to take in order to avoid checkmate—problems with the IRS:

- Save receipts.
- Make purchases with a credit card, debit card or checks from accounts used for business only.
- Save everything for five years.
- Get your tax preparer to burn a CD with your tax returns and all your records as a fail-safe backup strategy.
- Avoid cash purchases whenever possible.

Carry a combination of business and personal checks and/or credit cards with you all the time. The law is very simple on this point…the business owner decides whether or not the purchase is customary and appropriate for their business. If you are undecided, here's a simple question to ask yourself:

"If an employee was to bring me this receipt, would I reimburse them for the purchase?" In other words, can I support their decision? If the answer is yes then whip out the business Visa.

STRATEGY: Documentation is a "winning strategy." Don't let recordkeeping take you out of the game. There are simple, low-cost or no-cost minimal time solutions available.

FACT: Hire Your Family…get an additional refund up to $2,000+
Hiring your children and your spouse is another fabulous reason

why a home-based business adds great value to the family unit. Involving your children in your business teaches discipline, responsibility, work ethics and other skills. These skills will influence their work behavior in the future. A business shared with your spouse can be a boost for success.

A simple way to lower taxes is to split your income with family members by employing them in your business and paying them wages. The employment must be bona fide, and the pay must be reasonable for the services performed. Even a young child can be employed for cleaning the office, opening mail, mailing letters, filling orders, data input, washing the car...anything related to your business for which you would hire someone else.

Hire your children for say $10 per hour and have them work 40 hours each month. It's all tax free...so you write them a check for the full $400, and then deposit it into their personal bank account for which you happen to co-sign since they are underage.

This money can serve as a college fund or may be spent on business development. Since your children are in a lower tax bracket, this is an ideal way of conserving family funds. At year-end, you take a deduction for their payroll and increase your refund. It has to be a "real" payroll with all the normal business reporting. The good news is there are practitioners out there who have affordable turnkey services available to take care of all the paperwork for you.

STRATEGY: Do It Correctly; Get a Payroll Specialist.

FACT: Stop Taking Vacations.

Now that you have put your spouse and children on payroll, and they are an official part of your business, never take another vacation! Remember, portions of business trip expenses are a tax write off. Travel costs are deductible if they are "ordinary and necessary" for conducting your business. Trips to conventions, tradeshows, seminars, meetings with important clients, suppliers, business associates are all allowable deductions because they have a business purpose.

STRATEGY: Keep a Travel Log...Document Your Business Purpose.

FACT: The Biggest Key to Saving Taxes Is Your Ignition.

Most autos are used for both personal and business needs. The IRS requires you to maintain a simple log in order to determine the percentage of business vs. personal mileage. Filling out the record won't take as long as fastening your seat belt. And you only have to do it for 90 days. Keep a "Vehicle Use-Log" in your car. You only need to record four items each time you turn on the ignition: Date, odometer, destination and purpose. That's it. Destination and purpose don't need to be precise...just one or two words will do. Commuting is never deductible. However, travel from your home to a business destination can be deductible if your home qualifies as a place of business. The IRS's "Two Business Location Rule" states that you can deduct mileage driven from one business location to a second business location.

STRATEGY: Use the Two Business Location Rule to Maximize Mileage.

The bottom line is that there are great advantages to operating your own home-based business. But the treasure is in the records you keep. As an example, the IRS allows 40 cents for every mile of business travel. If you do not properly document that travel, it is as though you are throwing away a $20 bill for every 50 miles driven.

This is just a beginning of what tax saving deductions await the home-based business entrepreneur.

These tax strategies are for general information purposes only. To determine how this or any other tax information might apply to your specific tax situation contact an Enrolled Agent or other qualified, licensed tax professional.

RHONDA JOHNSON is managing partner of Accountable Solutions LLC, a diversified financial services company specializing in business tax preparation and direct sales motivation. Rhonda, a respected author, speaker, trainer, tax professional and networking diva, has been in the direct selling industry over 20 years. She has assisted hundreds to organize their offices, develop healthy work habits and maximize legitimate tax deductions, allowing them to keep more of what they make. Call Rhonda at (866) 282-3127, email her at Rhonda@accountablesolutions.biz or visit http://accountablesolutions.biz.

⌒

CHAPTER 18

Pay It Forward: Coaching for Success™

KAREN A. JONES, MA, MFT

AN (IRREVERENT) HISTORY OF PSYCHOLOGY

GRADUATE SCHOOL REQUIRED READING is quite like the brussel sprouts of the dinner plate: if you hold your nose and chew fast enough, dessert will inevitably follow. I remember snapping shut *Basic Writings of Sigmund Freud* and mimicking Moonstruck's Olivia Dukakis as she proclaimed to the womanizing professor, "What you don't know about women is a lot!"

I find it odd that psychoanalytic theory, basically inapplicable to over half the world's population, i.e., women, forms the ideological basis of what our society considers normal. But then again, the same can be said of the entire history of allopathic medicine. Yet, were it not for psychoanalysis and it's most lucrative offspring, the self-help genre, Oprah might still be doing radio in Nashville.

The great Spandex of our lifetime, the self-help revolution, has released and revamped powerful psychological and psychoanalytic principles from the confines of academic and clinical crypts into the bright daylight of women's lives. This is a good thing. But although we may have migrated from the psychoanalytic consulting offices into our own homes with books in hand or in front of our own TVs, we're still on the couch. Reflective of the American appetite, the glutinous self-help sections of major bookstores have taken Pac-Man-like glee in systematically gobbling up entire racks of literary masterpieces, giving new meaning to the phrase, "midlife spread." There now exists, quite literally, a self-help guide for every obscure ailment of contemporary life imaginable.

And the genealogy doesn't stop there. Just as psychoanalysis sired the psychological self-help movement, so the latter has given birth to the latest sensation, coaching. I recently met a woman who introduced herself as a homework coach. When I asked if that was anything like a tutor, she stated her role was not really to teach anything but to motivate children to do their homework. If there are two million self-help books, there are a million coaches. I should know... I am one of them.

PARADIGM SHIFT

After almost twenty years of practicing psychotherapy, I hit the books again and became a professional coach. Don't get me wrong, I loved my years as a psychotherapist and am proud of the great work done by my colleagues in the field. What I didn't love were the constraints placed on us by managed care, carve outs and the insurance industry. I was forced to diagnose what was wrong with my patients so that their sessions would be paid for, rather than nurturing what was right in order to move through psychological barriers. It was very freeing to strip away the clutches of managed care and insultingly poor insurance reimbursement and watch the beauty of my craft come alive again. That single paradigm shift was the emotional equivalent of shedding those last ten pounds. It just felt right.

The same paradigm shift has seemingly infiltrated corporate America as well. Savvy managers, supervisors and HR personnel are now working employees to their strengths instead of sending them off for remedial correction of their weaknesses. Hiring practices and performance reviews now demonstrate a holistic interest in employees, their intrinsic value, perceived job satisfaction and non-monetary compensation plans. When we stop looking for problems, the answers appear.

I believe this paradigm shift is partially responsible for the recent and considerable growth of the home-based business industry. Entrepreneurs are stepping out in droves to join network marketing, direct sales, franchising and MLM opportunities, carving out their slice of the American pie. Women in particular are beginning to believe they can have it all. They are evolving from "I'll believe it when I see it" to "I'll see it when I believe it." The shift is subtle, but the effects are amazing.

WHERE COACHING COMES IN FOR YOU

The majority of women reading this book will be part of the corporate world, own their own small business or operate a home-based business. Whether you are responsible for a department, a region or an empire, coaching is the ace up your sleeve that will take your group from good to great. With a little training and the right attitude, you can coach your teams to success. Certainly, you may require outside consultation to get started, but any good coaching system should encourage independence in its participants and develop over time a completely self-sustaining, turnkey operation, which is easily duplicated. In an abundant world, outside coaches should help you set up the systems, be there for booster shots and fine tuning, but then move out of your way as your internal coaching takes off.

The Pay It Forward: Coaching for Success System™ was designed to offer corporate business people, direct sellers and network marketers the same insights and strategies utilized by professional business and life coaches. This system will help you create rapid and lasting changes in personal and team performance and perceived personal and career satisfaction. It is all about paying forward a portion of your own experience, intuition and talents as investments in your team members. It is based on creating The Good Coach(es).

The Good Coach:
- holds a space for who we are becoming
- believes in us when we may not believe in ourselves
- sees the potential in our strengths
- reminds us that we will not always be where we are now
- challenges us to step out of our comfort zones
- reminds us of our dreams

The Good Coach employs the four fundamental tools of coaching:
- listening
- probing
- clarifying
- challenging
- empowering

The Good Coach teaches us how to set boundaries in ways that actually enhance relationships. The Good Coach reminds us that "No" is a complete sentence.

The beauty of peer or in-house coaching is that both participants (or all participants in group coaching) benefit from the implementation of this exciting process. The coach is kept accountable and growing, learns to duplicate herself and leverage her time, reduces her own stress by developing and supporting more people in less time, has more energy for her own goals, and experiences the satisfaction of helping others achieve their goals. The coaching recipient learns to shape her own vision, build confidence, resilience and success patterns, improve personal accountability and coach her own team. Both participants begin to develop the kind of loyalty that comes from a shared vision overcoming perceived barriers to success and self-defeating cognitive and behavioral patterns.

Have you ever been in a coaching situation in which you were unable to pinpoint what was holding someone back? In my experience, all coaching dilemmas boil down to a list of ten psychological issues, and I suggest you take this list with you into every coaching session. Once you know them, you are at a distinct advantage, and you'll be listening for the same cues as professional coaches. For example, a coaching recipient may report feeling "stuck." This may be her subjective feeling, but in truth, being stuck is impossible. What she's doing is making the very same choices over and over again. Being stuck is an active not passive process. The ticket is to look at what choices she is making consistently and explore what fears are keeping her from making different choices. Her identified challenges fall into one or more of ten universal underlying psychological themes:

- fear of failure
- fear of success
- fear of criticism
- fear of the unknown
- fear of change
- stepping out of one's comfort zone
- feeling unworthy
- fear of leaving others behind
- fear of exposure
- fear of stepping into one's full power

Here's where the fun really begins. This process shifts the locus of control back to the recipient who's had the answers all along. Now we're using psychological theory in women's best interest.

With confidence in her own inner knowing restored, the coaching recipient feels she too has something to pay forward.

The long-term benefits of coaching, as measured by perceived satisfaction and quantifiable performance enhancement, are huge. Most important to sustaining an organization of any size is coaching's contribution to the development of leadership. Leadership development is essential to belief and loyalty building—the foundation of stability and longevity. Henry Miller said it best:

"The only way anyone can lead us is to restore to us the belief in our own guidance."

KAREN A. JONES, MFT, psychotherapist and coach, is principal owner of Toolz of the Trade™: consultants in personal growth and business development. As a nationally recognized lecturer in behavioral change, team building and leadership training, she brings excitement to corporations and businesses. An award-winning philanthropist, Karen was South Coast's 1992 Woman of the Year and Laguna Beach's 1998 citywide proclamation recipient for HIV/AIDS activism. For Pay It Forward: Coaching for Success™ contact Karen: (949) 455-3200 or www.karenjones.com.

⌒

CHAPTER 19

The Net Wealth Woman

VALERIE LUNDEN, MA

UNBELIEVABLE, but it's not the cash money one accumulates in a savings account that matters, it's the total amount we are worth on paper that will save us through retirement. Net Wealth is a money concept related to assets accumulation. In 2000 my personal Net Wealth was approximately $10,000, the amount I had hoarded away in my retirement account at work. At that time I had already started to think about retirement, so as you might imagine this situation seemed dismal. Like many people, I paid rent and I had my fair share of debt, which I describe as paying someone else, not myself!

That year (2000), I was working part-time and my earnings were less than $30,000. I didn't know it then, but this was the beginning of my interest in the concept of Net Wealth. After months of research on the Internet, I discovered a first-time homeowner program that I qualified for and a mortgage lender who approved my loan. Looking back, I consider research, the Internet and a shift in thinking as the most important tools in my possession. English philosopher and lawyer Francis Bacon wrote that knowledge is power, and he certainly knew what he was talking about.

In contrast, today my Net Wealth is inching closer toward the one million mark, most of it accumulated in the last twenty-four months. As most billionaires might suggest, owning real estate and other assets remains the fastest and best way to improve Net Wealth. The main focus is to always buy low and sell high. However, this might seem next to impossible when real estate values are off the charts, the stock market indexes are virtually at the same place they were in 2004, and currency rates indicate that the dollar is worth half as much as it was three years ago. In fact the buzz around most financial coffee tables is when will the "bust" happen?

But whether you start accumulating Net Wealth today or wait for the economic downturn to come and go, what happens next remains a test of individual financial endurance. Just keep in mind there are always deals to be had and deals to be made. Again, always be cautious, investigate as much as possible, and try your best to understand all the financial implications.

So, what do women really want? Is it wealth? The best answer here is, yes! Yes, women should want wealth. They should want it more then a Gucci timepiece or a Mercedes, which in tax terms are considered not the best depreciating assets to own when building a Net Wealth portfolio.

To understand more about assets, think about either signing up for a tax class or playing the board game Cashflow (invented by Robert Kiyosaki and available at www.richdad.com). This fun game offers insight on how individuals think about and spend money. The goal of the game is to stop collecting paychecks, as most of us are in the habit of doing. The best alternative is to live off cash flow, the money left over after bills are paid, money is saved and additional assets/investments are accumulated. In real life this is how rich people live.

WHAT IF THE ONLY OBSTACLE
TO GAINING NET WEALTH IS YOU?

Let's face it, ladies, spending can be a thoughtless activity. There are so many ways to be pampered, and often we think nothing of the financial consequences. Buying a new dress, having a manicure, or even spending the night out having dinner or seeing a movie are activities done without thinking about where the money is going.

THE NET WEALTH TEST
THE FIRST CHANGE IS ATTITUDE

Do women actively create wealth?

This next statement may sound outrageous, but many people spend more time thinking about being poor than being rich. We are programmed to know more about spending than we do about saving. Knowing this, the question is, how can we change this preset way of thinking?

If the conscious Attitude is to be wealthy and we focus on the conscious Activities to make wealth happen, then it is more than likely the Adjustment to create a successful financial plan will be easier to manage. The same applies in reverse. If we plan not to be wealthy, (and the activity is to spend), then the adjustment will be proportionate to that activity, which is we won't become wealthy.

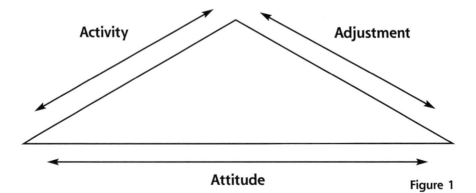

Activity   **Adjustment**

Attitude

Figure 1

The Performance Pyramid (Figure 1) applies to most every financial situation. There is no particular direction to take, and all outcomes are the same regardless of the circumstances. By following these three activities, with the intention of creating Net Wealth, it is possible to create abundance.

WEBSTER'S DEFINITIONS WITH QUESTIONS

ATTITUDE: POSTURE OR RELATIVE POSITION, FEELING, OPINION OR MOOD

What has been your past attitude toward creating Net Wealth? Are you ready to take the journey toward wealth or do you still need more time? If you are waiting, what are you waiting for? [This might be a good time to write down your answers!]

ACTIVITY: STATE OF BEING ACTIVE

What are you doing to improve your financial goals? Do you have a plan? What assets do you want to accumulate? What do you need to find out in order to make this happen?

ADJUST: FIX OR SET RIGHT?

What changes do you need to make? Stop spending? Start a budget? How much money do you actually need to live on? How much money do you need to set your financial goals in motion?

Before accumulating wealth, it might be important to discover why you are not accumulating wealth. As mentioned, most of us think poor. With this sort of attitude, accumulating Net Wealth can be a challenge rather than a way of life.

The end of this chapter provides a few resources to help you create wealth focus. Everyone has to walk before they can run, and choosing which path to take will be up to you. Keep in mind that accepting this challenge requires the right attitude, activities and adjustments.

LET'S CREATE NET WEALTH TOGETHER!

The following daily exercises are designed to create focus. You will need a notebook (nothing fancy). For today and the next ninety days, complete each exercise. Spend no more than five minutes on each exercise. Think quickly—write quickly. Remember that this is not a graded test. Start today!

On day ninety-one reread this chapter. Remember what you begin today will last a lifetime, and accumulating Net Wealth will become a habit—one that requires nurturing.

In addition, I have listed a few important books that offer financial knowledge. They can help promote a more focused attitude, activity and adjustment.

Your results are important and need to be shared. Please write to me, I would love to hear about your exciting journey on the road to Net Wealth.

NET WEALTH EXERCISE 1 (DAILY)

Write down five personal successes that you accomplished today.

NET WEALTH EXERCISE 2 (DAILY)

Repeat three times, each, out loud.
1. I want Net Wealth.
2. I create Net Wealth.
3. I learn about and research Net Wealth every day.

RECOMMENDED NET WEALTH READING:

Rich Dad, Poor Dad
Robert Kiyosaki

The ABC's of Building a Business Team That Wins
Blair Singer

The Millionaire Next Door
Thomas J. Stanley, Ph.D.
William D. Dankos, Ph.D.

The Richest Man in Babylon
George S. Clason

Think & Grow Rich
Napoleon Hill

Using the principles she teaches, VALERIE H. LUNDEN went from zero net worth to gaining INCREASED NET WEALTH in less than two years. She combines a unique blend of practical financial know-how with a whole lot of heart to help women and children reach their financial goals. Valerie was featured in the Los Angeles Times article, Low on Cash She Found a Good Place to Start. Email: info@brightperformance.com. Subscribe to Performance News, the FREE Wealth Building Newsletter designed for women on the go!

CHAPTER 20

Reach the Stars:

Make Goal-Setting Your Formula for Success

PAT LYNCH, Ph.D., SPHR

HOW MANY TIMES HAVE YOU SAID TO YOURSELF, "I want to do such-and-such some day?" Or "I really need to start that college fund for the kids?" Or "I know I need to get started on…!"

Goal setting is a process that can empower you to achieve your desired business and personal outcomes. Yet how many people do you know (including yourself) who can show you a list of their goals? In order to make the transition from "inspiration to realization," you must be able to state clearly where you want to go, how you are going to get there, and how you will know when you've arrived.

There are four major steps in the goal-setting process that are essential for your success. On the next few pages we'll discuss these strategies (and ways to avoid the most common mistakes that sabotage goal-setting efforts) so you can make goal-setting work successfully for you!

SUCCESS STRATEGY #1: CREATE A CLEAR PICTURE
OF WHAT YOU WANT

Begin with the end in mind—i.e. what specific outcomes do you want? For example, what does "having a successful business" mean to you? However you define it, be sure to focus on concrete results. Think of this strategy as painting a clear picture in your mind of what each goal will "look like" once you have achieved it.

How can you create these mental pictures? Effective goals are SMART goals—i.e., specific, measurable, achievable, results-oriented, time-bound. Incorporating all of these elements in each goal statement helps you say clearly what you really want to achieve. In addition to helping you paint a clear mental picture, they enable you to track your progress and indicate when you have arrived at your destination.

- Specific: use action verbs that conjure up a clear mental picture of the goal. Include only one "action" per goal so you can measure each outcome separately.

- Measurable: include ways to measure your progress and determine when you have reached your goal.

- Achievable: write realistic "stretch" goals. People are motivated to achieve challenging goals only when they are realistic.

- Results-oriented: focus on the specific outcome you desire, not the activities leading to that outcome.

- Time-bound: identify specific deadlines, including both dates and times.

Example: "Write a detailed business plan by 5 p.m. on November 1, 2005."

MISTAKES THAT CAN SABOTAGE GOAL-SETTING STRATEGY #1

While goals such as "increase my income," "work fewer hours," and "have a successful business" may sound good, they are too vague to be useful. Since you don't know what they actually mean, surely you won't be able to tell when you have achieved them! For example, if you make $1,000 more this year than last year or work 50 hours a week instead of 55, have you achieved your goals? Technically the answer is yes; in reality, these outcomes probably are not what you had in mind!

SUCCESS STRATEGY #2: DEVELOP BOTH "BIG PICTURE" AND "DAY-TO-DAY" GOALS

What does success "look like" to you? Each of us has a vision or a big picture of what we want in our business and personal lives. In order to realize that success, however, we need to identify the steps that will take us there. The secret to success is writing both "big picture" goals AND "day-to-day" goals. The big picture goals describe where we intend to go, our destination. They tend to be abstract and hard to measure, so we need the day-to-day goals to spell out the specific steps required for that journey.

Examples:

- Walk a marathon (big picture goal)
- Choose a marathon by July 30, 2005 (day-to-day goal)
- Join the Leukemia & Lymphoma Society's Team in Training program by August 6, 2005 (day-to-day goal)

MISTAKES THAT CAN SABOTAGE GOAL-SETTING STRATEGY #2

Consider the cases of Ellen and Sam, perpetual unsuccessful dieters. Because they don't understand there are two distinct kinds of goals that serve different purposes, they are very frustrated and discouraged with the goals they set. Ellen's only goal is to lose weight. Since this big picture goal doesn't tell her what she needs to do to lose the weight, Ellen is discouraged because the goal seems unmanageable. Sam has two goals: to keep track of what he eats and to weigh himself every Monday. Even though he may meet these goals, the fact that he has no big picture goal means that Sam is unable to answer the question "Am I there yet?"

SUCCESS STRATEGY #3: USE YOUR GOALS ON A DAILY BASIS

Are you familiar with the saying "Out of sight, out of mind?" It might serve as a reminder of this success strategy, which is that well-written goals can be an incredibly effective way to help you focus on your desired outcome. However, you must use your goals actively in order to reap their benefits.

Keep your goals in a highly visible place so you see them every day. Your big picture goals will inspire and motivate you to realize your vision. Your day-to-day goals will serve as a blueprint for action.

Refer to your day-to-day goals frequently to help you make focused decisions. Given the large number of exciting and interesting opportunities out there, it is critical to use your goals to help you choose the most effective path on your journey toward business and personal success.

Example: Assess potential projects, clients, speaking opportunities, membership in professional organizations, etc. by asking,

"Which goal does this opportunity support?" If the answer is "none," turn it down.

MISTAKES THAT CAN SABOTAGE GOAL-SETTING STRATEGY #3

How many times have you written goals, put them in a drawer, and forgotten about them? Failing to review your vision of success and implement your day-to-day goals is a sure way to sabotage your dreams.

SUCCESS STRATEGY #4: REVISE YOUR GOALS AS YOUR NEEDS CHANGE

Unless you are someone who has always known exactly what you want, your vision of business and personal success has evolved over time. When your desired outcomes or destinations change, it's time to revise your goals.

Re-evaluate your goals periodically to ensure they continue to serve your purposes. If your business is relatively new or changes rapidly, assess both your big picture and your day-to-day goals quarterly. If your business is more established and/or stable, evaluate your big picture goals once a year but continue the quarterly review of your day-to-day goals.

Give yourself permission to change your goals when they don't serve you any more. As an entrepreneur, you are your own boss. When your goals no longer serve the business and personal outcomes you envision, you don't need anyone's permission to change them.

Example: When I made the transition from academia to consulting, I went from a very structured environment in which my success was defined by various university stakeholders to a very unstructured environment in which I largely define my own success. It was time to throw out my old goals and start all over again!

MISTAKES THAT CAN SABOTAGE GOAL-SETTING STRATEGY #4

One of the biggest challenges entrepreneurs face is lack of time. Therefore when our needs or visions change, we are tempted to keep our existing goals or tweak them a little so we can get back to our "real" business. Just as we wouldn't change our travel destination without changing our flight plans accordingly, we need to recognize that failing to revise our goals when our desired outcomes change is a sure way to sabotage our results.

You can do it! Make goal setting work successfully for you by setting clear goals for both the big picture and day-to-day, by using your goals in daily decision-making, and by changing your goals when they no longer serve your needs. Following these strategies will keep you focused on your journey to business and personal success and help you reach the stars!

PAT LYNCH, PH.D., SPHR, author, trainer and consultant, is an expert in human resource management. Her consulting practice, HR Value, is based on Pat's conviction that successful entrepreneurs achieve their goals when they can demonstrate and communicate the value of their work to decision-makers. In her spare time, Pat walks marathons for the Leukemia and Lymphoma Society and is a mentor for its Team in Training marathon walk program. You can reach her at Pat@HRValue.biz.

CHAPTER 21

⌒

Strategic Alliances: Wonder Twin Power! Activate!

ALISON MACPHERSON

WONDER WOMAN. She's OUR superhero. When a woman embarks on a new venture, like starting her own business, Wonder Woman is who we strive to become. We envision ourselves arriving on the scene in our invisible airplane suddenly and single-handedly saving the day.

But in today's world, success need not be achieved single-handedly. Perhaps you remember The Wonder Twins. These super-heroes were two ordinary people...until they joined their fists in the air and transformed into an eagle and waterfall, or a tiger and a tower of ice. You don't have to be Wonder Woman to be a super-hero. All you need is someone with whom to join forces. Through strategic alliances, two people can help each other transform their business into entities larger than the two of them combined.

Coming to this realization has been more valuable to me than any "secret weapon." I wish I could say it was the result of my supernatural business acumen. But in truth, it merely grew out of my natural curiosity; I wanted to find out what other people in my field were doing and how they became successful. In short, I knew

I needed to link with other like-minded people. Soon enough I discovered people were interested in more than just sharing advice. They had business needs I could help them execute. Happily, the reverse has been true as well. Several exciting strategic alliances have been born.

Simply put, a strategic alliance is a partnership between two business entities (or business associates) that mutually enhances both parties. Strategic alliances can be formal or informal arrangements, and they can exist for one particular venture or across several business avenues. Joining forces with a partner can increase your revenue streams, your ability to service a current client, as well as enable you to win new business or service it faster. Today's market requires a global presence or a footprint in a foreign country, and alliances can give you that presence and visibility.

Let me give you an example. In my clinical trials business, I help pharmaceutical companies test their medication before it gets FDA approval. I developed an alliance with "Jane" who provides business development support for doctors who conduct clinical research. When Jane finds out about pharmaceutical companies in need of assistance in the clinical trials realm, she relays those leads to me. And when I learn of doctors in need of business development support, I refer those leads to Jane. She's signed business from leads I've given and vice versa. Jane and I have a verbal contract.

I have a more formal alliance with a group in the UK. They provide similar services to what my company offers. But this company needs feet on the ground in the US, which I am able to provide. Our agreement is sealed by a formal contract that will expire when the project concludes.

I now actively seek out new strategic alliances for my businesses, one of which is an advertising agency. The alliances with my advertising group that have worked best so far are with a PR firm, a promotions group, and a high tech creative company. These alliances are in their infancy, yet we've already pitched, and won, a few clients together.

How do you go about forming one of these magical alliances? First, you'll want to identify the companies you'd be best suited to partner with. Finding them requires some research and willingness to make some missteps. Start by answering these questions: When thinking of your own business growing and expanding, which new markets do you want to tap into? Is it a different region, a different type of clientele, or adding a service to your roster? If you create a list of potential businesses or people to ally with, you may discover there are more options than you originally thought. Brainstorming with other business owners or creative thinkers who aren't in your industry is a great way to discover new methods of growing your business.

Next, you'll want to broach the subject of forming an alliance. Start out by suggesting ways you may be able to leverage their capabilities. It helps to meet in person to learn all you can about your potential partner, their work ethic, and their choice clients. Remember, you are in the exploration phase; a relationship develops over time, so dip your toes in the water first, as opposed to jumping in the deep end right away.

Some of your alliance opportunities will fall by the wayside because you or your partner won't nurture them. That's fine... maybe the timing isn't right, or maybe the business isn't there to support the relationship. Sometimes you may find you are throwing them more new clients than you receive. It's important not to keep a scorecard. What comes around goes around...and there will be times that you find yourself rife with opportunities from them.

If your business requires that you formalize arrangements with a legal document, be sure to consult your attorney. If there is money changing hands under the auspices of the joint venture, it should always be in writing. Verbal agreements that involve an exchange of money are trouble in the making. A formal written contract gives all parties a chance to confirm what they want out of the partnership, and what the parameters of the agreement are. It also gives you a chance to confine the scope of the alliance right from the start. As the relationship matures, you will want to add on to your shared venture.

Keep a written record of your alliances. Note when the collaboration started, what leads and prospects you've received, how it has beefed up your contact database, which business you pitched together or as a result of the partnership, and what revenue was gained and stood to be won. Regularly assess the partnerships and their viability. Clean house as needed and make these decisions quickly. If the alliance doesn't take any of your time or money or intrude on your contacts in any way, consider keeping it intact even if you aren't building your business through it. Assess the risks and the benefits objectively at least twice a year, or more often, depending on your business cycle.

When alliances haven't worked, I found out quickly. Be choosy about whom you link with. Monitor their professionalism, responsiveness, and interactions. Ask yourself: Is this person representing me and my business well? Do they share my business ethic? Is this venture leveraging my ability to compete? It's never too late to pull the plug as long as you don't leave your client in the lurch. Help your alliance subcontract with a suitable vendor or find a way to work the contract through to a sensible stopping point so your individual relationship with the client is preserved.

Stay in regular contact with all companies you partner with, no matter how active the business deals are. They are a trusted source of information about your industry, what concerns are on clients' minds, and trends to be aware of. Keep an eye out for information they may find useful. Sharing industry resources (blog links, trade publication articles, and newsletters) will be appreciated and hopefully reciprocated.

Partnerships aren't just for your business life. Negotiating with family and friends to baby-sit can win you an extra "date night," and your reciprocation makes for a compelling "win-win." Partnering with neighbors makes our communities more close-knit and can make our lives richer, easier, and more rewarding. Form strategic alliances in every area of your life. And before you know it, you'll be right in the center of your very own Super Friends Network.

ALISON MACPHERSON is the president and owner of Bright Pharmaceutical Services and Bright Media Services. She founded both companies in 2002 to focus on the needs of niche biotech and pharmaceutical research projects and to specialize in patient recruitment challenges. Bright Media has since expanded to become a full-service advertising agency. In 2001, Macpherson was elected to the Board of Big Brothers Big Sisters. She resides in Sherman Oaks, California and can be reached at alison@brightps.com or (818) 981-9100, www.brightps.com — www.brightmediaservices.com

⌒

CHAPTER 22

Start Now: Six Steps to Manifesting Your Dreams

LIN MOREL, MA, DSS

A DREAM IS DEFINED by Webster's Dictionary as "A visionary idea or fancy." The purpose of this chapter is to help you learn to pay attention and explore your visionary ideas. The following story contains the six steps that will help you make your dreams come true.

While I was spending my last day of vacation with a friend at a restaurant in Santa Barbara, she asked me a question that challenged my life.

"So Lin," she asked. "What is your dream?"

Buying time, I dipped my egg roll in mustard sauce. "I don't know." The reply came hesitantly, and the feeling was one of being caught on a quiz show and quite clueless.

"What do you mean?"

"Well," she said. "If you could do anything in the world, what would that be?"

"Don't know...I haven't thought about it," I replied.

"For example," she said. "If you wanted to start a business, what would you do?"

"Oh," I said, connecting to some part of me deeply buried and yearning to be born, "I'd be a stress management consultant and help people learn to live from a place of spiritual connection."

"That's great. How would you do that?"

Warming to the conversation, the talk turned to my martial arts training. "It's a tai chi principle. When we come from our center, that still small place within us, we can handle anything that comes our way. Our intuition and intention will guide us through the rough times as well as the good times."

Next she said, "Just for the fun of it, why not write your ideas down?"

Liking the notion, I started brainstorming ideas on the back of a placemat.

Three hours later, I settled in for the long flight home on a 747 bound for Newark. I grabbed the US Airways magazine and soon found myself laughing at an article on education. The woman next to me asked what was so funny. We got to talking, and she asked THE question. "What do you do?"

"Oh," I answered. "I'm a stress management consultant."

"Hmmm," she replied. "What sorts of things do you talk about?"

Shocked at my boldness, I proceeded to tell her what I had written down earlier.

"That sounds just like what our department needs. Do you have a business card?"

"No, not with me," I replied.

"No matter," she said. "What do you charge?"

Time stood still; my hands grew clammy. Out of my mouth, independent of logic, came a figure, followed by "plus expenses."

"Great," she said. "Do you know off hand if you are available on September 18?"

Time slowed itself once more as I asked myself if I could get a day off from work. "My schedule is at the office, but it seems as though that date will work fine."

"Wonderful," she said. "Here's my phone number, let's settle this tomorrow." Three hours after I declared a dream, I was hired by the Penfield School District in Rochester, New York.

THE SIX STEPS
FOR MANIFESTING YOUR DREAMS

STEP ONE: IDENTIFY YOUR DREAM

The Random House Dictionary defines intention as "the end or object intended." To get to "the end," we need a starting point. To identify your dream (the start) ask yourself, "What do you want?" This is frequently the most challenging step of all! Sometimes we need to know what we don't want before we can discover what we do want. Don't despair; your dream is safely tucked in your heart, ready for germination in its own timing.

When my window of opportunity opened, I found myself able to act because I had become truthful about what I wanted to do with my life. It was enough that my truth was shared with one person and scribbled on the back of a placemat. That simple first step of planting my dream was all I needed. The power of intention was set in motion.

STEP TWO: BE WHO YOU ARE

The second step toward making my dream come true, and the opening for me to express my authentic self, came through laughter. That led to connection and relationship with the woman who sat next to me. When we are radiant with laughter, joy and happiness, people are automatically attracted to us. We become magnets that pull in the perfect people and resources we need to manifest our dream. What we sow (or show) we reap. Your dream is an extension of your self. Trust that you are enough.

STEP THREE: PAY ATTENTION AND TAKE ACTION

Paying attention and taking appropriate action is crucial for success. When the door of opportunity opens, walk through! If you miss an opportunity, just let it go. There will be others. Don't waste your time in remorse.

Take a quick quiz. How many times a day are you living in the past (thought) or planning for the future (think)? While we may draw inspiration from the future and wisdom from the past, neither of these activities puts us in the moment. Paying attention is possible only when we are totally engaged and observing what is happening "in the now." Competitive martial arts taught me this. Pay attention or get hit. Sometimes our hits are financial, physical or emotional. Our universe gives us plenty of clues and feedback.

STEP FOUR: OBSERVATION FREE FROM JUDGMENT

My initial observation was that of delight mixed with trepidation. My heart celebrated my newfound boldness as my mind cringed at moving into the unknown territory of new beginnings.

It seems, in retrospect, that the bigger our dream, the less likely you will have a clue about how to proceed. I think that is a big bonus! It is easy to get bogged down with all we do not know and judge our progress. You can always figure out a small next step. Stay focused on that step. String enough steps together, and you will give birth to your dream.

STEP FIVE: LEARN AS YOU GO

I had only six weeks to plan for that workshop. My dining room table was piled high with books on stress management, my legal pad crammed with notations. In the end, I discovered a marvelous truth about preparation. It is a ladder, that once climbed, can be set aside. As I walked into that classroom, I put aside that ladder and shared from my heart. My dream was alive. All was well.

Dreams exist in our heart and are waiting to born when we say yes. Mistakes are a natural part of life. Those who learn, survive. Excellence, not perfection, is the key to survival and manifesting your dream.

STEP SIX: GRATITUDE

Gratitude is a door through which happiness and joy enter. What you focus on, you attract. In times of worry or anxiety, a strong habit of gratitude opens your heart and allows you to expand in the face of adversity. Gratitude will help you turn obstacles into stepping stones. Look for opportunity in every challenge, and you will see with new eyes. Grace and ease become your companion.

IN CONCLUSION

Set your intention today! Dare to dream BIG. Show up for yourself, pay attention to what makes you happy and what drains you of your energy. Take actions that feed your body, mind and spirit. Become an active observer-participant in your life. Do more of what works and less of what does not work. Practice gratitude in all your affairs.

I encourage you to release the belief that we must "work on our self" before we can be our Self. Our Self is the very thing that dreams are made of. Now get busy and make your dreams come true.

DR. LIN MOREL has spent twenty years helping individuals and groups move beyond stress into profound connection with their core strength and intuition. She teaches them to apply spiritual principles from the world's wisdom traditions, blended with the cutting edge dynamics of quantum physics, so they can show up, pay attention and use their intention to build greater health, wealth and happiness. Free gift at www.linmorel.com or to book her for an event, call (866) 305-4363.

CHAPTER 23

Branding For Your Soul

WENDY NEWMAN, MA

WOULD YOU RATHER BE RICH OR HAPPY? Would you settle for both?

My new client was pleading on the phone. "I have to sell 50,000 books a month starting next month! Tell me what to do!" This author and emerging personality sounded unhappy and stressed. During the next few sessions, I took her through my therapeutic marketing technique, which I sometimes call "branding for the soul," to bring her back to why she was doing this work in the first place…to make a difference in the lives of children. She had become so intent on demonstrating her success to her investors that she had forgotten her calling. When we shifted back to what was in her heart, she was not only happier, but her books started selling.

Traditional marketing and branding is externally focused. Can it work? Yes. So why not just do that? Because short-term success doesn't guarantee long-term results or happiness.

The tools in this chapter can help you change your life as they have for the numerous individuals and companies I've worked with over the years. Person-Centered Branding® (PCB) is an inside-out approach that helps you match your inside (who you really are) with your outside (what you present to the world) to create sustainable, lifetime results.

THE PERSON-CENTERED B-R-A-N-D

BELIEFS: One of my clients is an actress and has a day job in sales. She had wanted a job that would provide a steady income, didn't require travel away from her family, and would give her the flexibility to pursue her acting. After a number of years, she became upset at never being number one in any area of her life. Together we discovered an old belief system operating, that she "should" be number one—anything less meant she was a failure. This belief created an unnecessary struggle and JUDGMENT she had been carrying around about herself.

If you find yourself using words like "right and wrong," "good and bad," or in this case "should," you are probably stuck in judgment. Many of our BELIEF SYSTEMS are judgmental, irrational and unconscious, and they influence the decisions we make each day. I call these belief systems STEALTH OPERATING SYSTEMS (SOS) because they function under the radar of conscious thought.

My client and I began our work by first identifying and ultimately RELEASING JUDGMENTS she held against herself and others in order to create more space in her life for happiness and success. Once she was feeling more grounded and peaceful, I worked with her to REFRAME the idea of "number one" to "one of a kind" because she left such a distinct mark on everything she did. She came to the realization that she had made CHOICES to set up the life she'd wanted at the time, to honor her priority of providing a loving, stable home for her children. Now that her children are grown and she has opted to make different choices, her acting career has taken off!

RESPONSIBILITY. I was working with a senior level advertising executive who was bitter about a business deal that had fallen apart. He felt "screwed over" by his client. His body was charged up, and he was visibly upset.

I told him IF ANYTHING DISTURBS YOUR PEACE, IT IS ABOUT YOU, about something inside of you that still requires some inner work. I suggested he take PERSONAL RESPONSIBILITY for his thoughts, words and actions. He asked why he should make that commitment if the other person was unwilling to do so.

As we probed the matter more deeply, it became clear that what was mirrored back to him was a long-standing fear of being taken advantage of, as he perceived he had been as a child. He recognized that he had made an ASSUMPTION and that his client's INTENTIONS were never to cause any harm.

Each time you make an assumption about what someone else is thinking or doing, you prohibit yourself from being PRESENT to what is really happening and how your behavior may have contributed to the outcome.

Accepting his role in what happened helped my client see the benefits of taking responsibility. He has since resolved his inner conflict, has a better relationship with his client, and has experienced a major increase in revenue from that client's business.

AUTHENTICITY. After many years of success, my client, a well-known media personality, was witnessing all of his sponsorships and television deals falling apart. "What's happening to me?" he wanted to know.

The answer: He wasn't being his authentic self. The image he so carefully cultivated over the years was not the person he truly was.

First we explored what gives him "JUICE" in his work—what excites him about it. You are going to be more successful if you're doing what you love. CHECK IN WITH YOUR BODY; differentiate your head from your heart. When your energy rises, you are probably doing something you enjoy. What are you feeling when you're doing (or imagining) what you love versus doing something because you "have to"?

Then I suggested he ask the question, "WHAT VALUE DO I CREATE for myself and others through my work?" Once you know the value, lead with it. Your willingness to SPEAK YOUR TRUTH and ASK FOR WHAT YOU WANT also increases the odds that you will achieve an authentic outcome that has personal and even financial value for yourself and others!

Finally, he saw this OBSTACLE AS AN OPPORTUNITY—time to make a change. Often the biggest challenges in your life are gifts and a chance to raise the bar with regard to your personal and professional growth. He is now a multi-millionaire signing deals with companies who represent who he truly is, and he is also the happiest he has ever been.

N ICHE. One of my clients found her income (and her energy) continuing to drop. When we met, she actually thought it was time to find new work. We uncovered she was doing what she was passionate about, but there were parts of her work she didn't enjoy. Not only didn't she follow through with them, but they were also stopping her from moving forward in other areas of her life.

Once we found people who enjoyed these areas to assist her, she was rejuvenated, made more money than ever before (for both herself and the company she worked for), and even had time for an active social life.

The lesson is: FIND YOUR NICHE! What makes you and what you do unique? Capitalize on that!

D REAM. An attorney client who bought and sold properties found herself caught up in the money and deal making and had lost touch with her goal of helping people by creating affordable housing. She asked me, "How will I ever reach my dream?" She didn't know "how" to connect making money with doing what she loves.

I suggested she ask herself: "What is one small thing I can do today to move myself closer to my dreams?" LOSING THE "HOW," which can be overwhelming, and setting REALISTIC, ACHIEVABLE GOALS, no matter how small, inspires you to build upon your successes.

My client soon began attracting deals that presented opportunities she never thought were possible. As I write this, she has just signed contracts that will fulfill her dream of helping others while generating more than a million dollars in revenue!

So, let me rephrase this—DREAM BIG! And remember to START SMALL.

You are capable of making your dreams come true! I invite you to utilize these tools, revisiting the ones in CAPS, to take dominion over your life and create the life you want NOW! Remember—the Person-Centered Brand starts and ends with YOU. YOU can be rich, happy and make a difference in this world for others and for YOU!

Person-Centered Branding® . . .
one hand on your bottom line, one hand on your heart ...

WENDY NEWMAN, M.A. is the founder of Person-Centered Branding®, a process she developed in working with high profile corporate and entertainment executives, celebrities, professional athletes, radio and television personalities, kids and teens, entrepreneurs and professionals. She has helped them become not just millionaires, but happy and fulfilled ones. Newman resides in Beverly Hills with her husband, daughter and eighty pound lap dog, all co-founders of Heart-Centered Business^{SM}, dedicated to growing business from a heartfelt place. www.personcenteredbranding.com, wendy@personcenteredbranding .com, (310) 277-2200.

CHAPTER 24

Seven Steps to Empowered Wealth

An Entrepreneur's Blueprint for Financial Freedom

LYNN PIERCE

WOULD YOU LIKE TO WIN THE LOTTERY and have an instant millionaire's bank account? Silly question, right? More money is a good thing, and a lot more money is even better. But empowered wealth goes way beyond simply acquiring massive amounts of cash. Empowered wealth is the difference between having money and having the knowledge to create financial freedom. It's the blueprint for building a successful business and the life of your dreams.

Empowered wealth allows you to not only keep the fortune you acquire, but make the intelligent informed decisions required to maintain and build it.

STEP ONE: DISCOVER YOUR PASSION

True happiness comes from living your passion. I help women discover their passion and life purpose every day, and yes, you have a life purpose. Once you find it, then create a vision for your life and develop products from the topic you are passionate about.

Your vision is the script to the movie of your life, your screenplay so to speak. If you're going through life with only a vague idea of what you want your life to look like, you will never see it materialize. Without a vision for your life, your friends, family, co-workers, the media-basically everyone else but you is creating your screenplay.

Ultimately you want to be in business for yourself and create income while you sleep. If you are in a professional services industry, coach or consultant, you really need to develop product. There are only so many hours in a day that you can bill, and only so much your clients will pay. That's where product sales come in. You will never acquire the level of wealth that's available to you as long as you're trading hours for dollars.

STEP TWO: DEVELOP A WEALTH ATTITUDE

Be ready to receive large amounts of money when it comes to you. One of the biggest reasons people don't have financial freedom is because of their beliefs about what money represents and their worthiness to have it. To change this situation requires overcoming any self-limiting beliefs you may have. People who have empowered wealth live these eleven secrets to super success.

1. Take responsibility for your life.
2. Be a well-informed and intelligent risk taker.
3. Recognize your fears and overcome them.
4. Have a passion that drives you.
5. Set big, outrageous goals.
6. Create opportunities for yourself.
7. Know you always have choices.
8. Make your money work for you.
9. Make your life an adventure.
10. Enjoy the journey.
11. Work from the inside out.

Claim your free copy of the success action guide, "11 Secrets of Super Success" at www.SuccessBuildingSecrets.com

STEP THREE: BECOME AN EXPERT IN YOUR FIELD

Read a minimum of one book a month on your topic of specialization. Read at least one magazine or newsletter a month to stay on the cutting edge of your profession. Just imagine how different your life will be a year from now when you have read and implemented this additional information. This alone could make you an expert in your field compared to over 95 percent of your peers who never do any kind of reading or continuing education in their profession unless it's required by law.

Of course, implementation is the key. A good tip is to read and take notes as if you had to teach the material. You'll learn on a much deeper level.

Attend events that are peripheral to your business or events you have attended before just to network. Go where you think your target market can be found. Increase your list and make alliances with people to do joint ventures.

Make separate lists in your database for every event you attend so you can contact people with announcements of interest to them based on the topic of the event. Write an ezine to keep people informed on what's happening in your business.

Above all, get a coach or mentor to help you stay on track. You need to be accountable to someone other than yourself, your family and friends. An outside person can push you when you need to be pushed. Nothing great happens as big or as fast when you do it alone.

STEP FOUR: BECOME A MASTER PRODUCT PRODUCER

Having a product line instantly creates credibility and adds to your expert status. Creating products is much easier than you think.

I teach my infopreneurship students how to easily create a seminar or an eight CD audio/workbook program in a weekend or less. It is possible to create a $500 product in one day or less without writing a word! You probably have everything you need in your office right now.

STEP FIVE: EMBRACE EMPOWERED WEALTH PRACTICES

It takes several factors to make you a person of empowered wealth. When you embrace all ten practices, you can become a dramatically different person in as few as thirty days from now.

1. Daily spiritual practice
2. Develop high self-esteem
3. Consistently read books and listen to audio programs
4. Attend life-enhancing seminars
5. Find mentors to speed your growth
6. Create a mastermind group
7. Maintain positive thoughts about yourself and the world
8. Commit to live your life to its fullest
9. Turn dreams into goals with a plan
10. Step fully into your power

STEP SIX: BECOME A MASTER COMMUNICATOR

The secret to becoming a master communicator is how you have the conversation.

Conversation: an oral exchange of sentiments, observations, opinions or ideas. The key is exchange. A conversation involves at least two people actively participating. In many sales situations there is only one person talking.

Whether you are a businessperson, a parent or a spouse, you're in sales. All day long you are involved in situations where you are trying to get to yes with someone. Whether you're talking to clients, vendors or your kids or doing marketing or networking, in every situation you have a desired outcome that leads to yes.

The deciding factor in whether you can get to yes without selling or not in each of these situations is the way you have the conversation. No tricks involved. Straightforward conversation.

Sales is one of those love/hate things. But let me ask you something. What's the difference in how you feel after making a two-hour presentation to a client and a two-hour conversation with a friend?

One leaves you drained while the other leaves you energized, right? It's not about who you're talking to; it's about how you're doing it. Too much selling and too much talking leave you drained because you're not having a conversation.

When you leave with more energy than you started with, it's because of how the conversation was handled on many different levels. You can achieve this level of communication with anyone. It's easy. I've been teaching people from all walks of life how to do this for over twenty-five years!

STEP SEVEN: BE A LIFE-LONG LEARNER

Wealthy people are continually learning. Read constantly. Listen to educational CD's. Attend seminars. Network and build your sphere of influence. Acquire the tools you'll need to build your business before you need them so you're prepared when opportunities arise. Have a plan and take action daily.

Empowered wealth means having savings and investment programs. Your rate of return will be based on how much time and money you are willing to spend to get it. You have a choice if you put your money in the bank at one to three percent, or if you will learn to consistently get fifteen to twenty-five percent return. Wealthy people spend the time and money required to build their fortune, preserve it and have their money work for them.

Implement the seven secrets to empowered wealth in your daily life, and you can join the ranks of the truly wealthy.

LYNN PIERCE, founder of "Women's Business Empowerment Summit," is a recognized sales expert and creator of "Getting to YES Without Selling, The YES System" and "Infopreneurship for Women Only." With twenty-five years in sales and thirty years studying human behavior, Pierce helps clients pull more cash out of what they're already doing. She offers comprehensive services producing immediate results. Email her at Lynn@LynnPierce.com or call (480) 242-5929 Visit www.GettingToYesWithoutSelling.com for a free mini-course.

⌒

CHAPTER 25

How to Start a Business with Your Head...and Your Heart

KELLEY REXROAD

NOT LONG AGO, I found myself near the top of the corporate ladder but up against the wrong building.

I loved my job, but I was tired of going through the same motions. In fact, I was just tired due to lots of travel, a 24/7 workforce and things and people were bothering me that hadn't before—people with hidden agendas, insincere actions and talking.

I was waking up at night worrying, not wondering. It was time to do something else. I considered consulting, but I did not want it to be the rebound lover. What were my goals and how would I get there? What was special about my consulting? Was I a commodity? Did I have a value? Did I have an idea that people would pay for? I didn't know what I didn't know.

I decided to look at my head and my heart. I will share my journey, hoping it will help you.

YOUR HEAD

First, I took some time off and read. I read lessons learned, books on how to start a business, biographies on those who sorted out their lives and had started businesses. I listened to tapes and CDs helping me to understand who I was, and why I wanted and perhaps needed, to go in this direction. I found the worn Earl Nightingale tapes almost new in my ears. My reading gave me time for my head to clear. I read on the quiet, sunny dock on the lake. It was a sanctuary and a wonderful place to pause.

It was there I learned about a USP. What was my Unique Selling Proposition? I read Seth Godin, Alan Weiss, Elaine Biech, Raleigh Pinskey, Jack Trout, Jay Levinson, Michael Gerber and more. I read more than 100 books in the first few months. I am sure the UPS man wonders if I have stock in Amazon.

During this time, my folks came to visit. I spent five weeks with them, walking parks, doing day trips, gardening. I was eighteen the last time I spent that much time with them. It was a very special time, and it renewed our relationship in a way I can't even describe.

I took classes at the Small Business Development Center. The classes were good; the expertise was amazing, but the enthusiasm of other classmates is what kept me going.

I listened to other consultants. Confident competitors shared their thoughts. I met with some who were not in the same line of consulting as myself as well as vendors.

Some say you must be a little bit crazy to go into business for yourself. I agree. Get professional help, but I mean a lawyer and an accountant. Create a Board of Advisors who will help you. Get people who challenge your thinking.

Do a business plan, even as a sole proprietor. The business plan should be put together and read, changed, read and changed. It is your living document. Your USP should flourish throughout it. The business plan format is available through books, software and free information on the Internet. The planning and deliberate questions you must answer will help you in the long run.

Put together a marketing plan. Who is your target market? Is the market today the same as last year? A friend asked me a very clarifying question: "What does your ideal client look like?"

Have your financials together. How long can you do this? Are you ready to give up a steady paycheck-at least at the beginning? It is more than balancing the checkbook. Plan for the unexpected. Companies go out of business due to lack of cash; not lack of work. Planning will give you confidence.

You will need tools, and this means expenses: a computer, software and supplies. Where will you work? Is the dining room table appropriate? I work from a home office -and it has been a challenge bringing home twenty-four years' worth of a career at (gratefully, bigger and bigger) offices.

You can make a career and go broke by joining organizations. I narrowed it down to a few in my marketing plan. I subscribe to magazines and newspapers. Be sure to get the *Business Journal* in your local area. They have daily alerts which come out each workday and give you a heads up on the business news. There are also many free ezines.

Consulting is you. Your brand is your image and promise. Think about what your card, your message and your material looks like; how it feels. I engaged an expert. I knew if I was to consult with senior executives I needed a card and material of quality. I consistently get comments on how wonderful my material looks, reads and feels. Get a website. I started with some general information, my email address and phone number. (By the way, a PO Box is okay). The domain name is key. Starting your business is no place for dancingrabbit@beachbunny.com. Is that the image you want your customer to have of you and your business?

Professional development is important. Participate in conferences and teleseminars. Office Depot has a wonderful small business section and offers a web café. Each teleseminar is an opportunity to learn and an opportunity to get your name out there. As you introduce yourself-say it with energy and a smile.

There are more opportunities for visibility. Write Letters to the Editor. One letter I wrote became Letter of the Week in the *The Tampa Tribune* and has been picked up on several other web sites. (My Google alerts told me that.)

Write for newsletters and books like this one. Speak for groups, your church or temple, scouts or a retiree home. Susan Roane's advice on acting like a host at events certainly helped me break the ice.

During my corporate life, my volunteer time was limited. I gave more money than time. Now, I have more time than money, so I volunteer. Every two weeks for about two hours, I give my platelets, a life saving blood product. I also conduct "Get Ready for Work" workshops for adults and young adults looking to enter or trying to re-enter the workforce.

YOUR HEART

The questions from your heart are not as many; but they are bigger.

- *Do you really want to do this?* Do you smile when you think of doing your own thing? Are you excited and scared? Do you think more about this than a "real" job? Do you want to be a consultant or just want to be one until something real comes along?

- *Do you have the discipline?* In the corporate world, my calendar was filled every day with meetings, and now the calendar is mine. It started empty-and that was scary.

- *Do you have the support of your family?* Do they understand you will be so filled with passion again, that they may even be jealous? Do they understand you can't do the dishes, laundry, groceries and have dinner ready and work your consulting job? As your own boss, you have flexibility.

ARE YOU READY?

Have you convinced your head and do you have enough heart to go forward? You shouldn't have to convince your heart. "If you have to think about it," my Granny said, "you probably shouldn't do it." To be in business for yourself, you need both your head and your heart.

I worked very hard for other peoples' companies. I was known for integrity, results, customer service and tenacity.

Now, I enjoy working as hard for myself and my clients as I did for those firms.

I know this is right. I sleep well at night and don't wake up worrying. Instead I wake up wondering, what if?

Human Resources and communications expert KELLEY REXROAD, SPHR, is a consultant, author and speaker. Her twenty-five years of experience and education gives her the ability to drill down to the true issues, allowing her to coach people and organizations to reach their potential. She is known as a "big company expert with front porch common sense" solving people issues with business strategies. Reach her through www.krexconsulting.com or kelley@krexconsulting.com. By phone: (813) 920-9030.

CHAPTER 26

⌒

Creating Success:
Your Life, the Ultimate Tool Kit
CHENOA SMITH

It is always our conscious choice which secret garden we will tend... when we choose not to focus on what is missing from our lives but are grateful for the abundance that's present— love, health, family, friends, work, the joys of nature and personal pursuits that bring us pleasure—the wasteland of illusion falls away and we experience Heaven on earth.

—SARAH BAN BREATHNACH

YOUR LIFE IS A TOOL KIT. In this tool kit, there are lots of experiences, joys, pains, learned skills, epiphanies and deep insights. Your tool kit is made for you to discover your destiny. Your tool kit is designed as an information source for other people to use in their journey and so on. What would the world be like if one person hadn't decided to advocate that walls were a good idea? The concept of a wall started with one person with a unique series of experiences and needs a long, long time ago.

You have the best opportunity at the beginning of a business to question, understand, and then, manifest your vision by both connecting with the right people *and* using the best business tools. The first connection with the "right people" is to understand your history and yourself. Let's make a journal for reviewing these experiences so you will have your personal inventory to manifest your business.

YOUR WORK HISTORY

Let's think about the many bosses you have had over the years. You probably remember a few things about them. First, I'm sure you remember the task you were assigned to do for them as part of your job. I'm sure you also remember complaints you had. You may even remember needed improvements in the products or services the business offered. Those needed improvements may have been the working environment or benefits. Remembering those things clears lessons for you in your current business endeavors. They are part of the grand evolution that we are experiencing together every day in business along with our personal, emotional, mental, family and spiritual lives.

When many people think about their work history, they focus on why their former bosses/employees were incompetent, uncaring, inadequate, etc. These types of thoughts waste up to 90 percent of our thinking energy. The reality of the situation is however, despite their faults and shortcomings, these organizations did meet the needs of their customers. Period. They also are competitive. These organizations do AT LEAST ONE THING BETTER THAN EVERYONE ELSE.

This means that the organization has figured out how to be a leader in one particular area, even if it is providing warm cookies to customers upon every visit. In most circumstances, the organizations you have worked for have done more than one thing better than everyone else in meeting a particular customer group's needs. What needs does your business meet with its products or services? How effective is the delivery of those products or services? How does your business work relative to others?

REMEMBERING YOUR PARENTS

Believe it or not, your parents gave you some amazing gifts. Let's start from the beginning. Let's remember your mother. Picture her in your head. What were her key traits? Was she an organization freak? Did she teach you how to cook? Did she read certain books? Did she have a certain way of commanding attention that was effective? Did she have a particular laugh? What kind of work did she do or hobbies did she have?

Now, let's remember your father. Picture him in your head. What were his key traits? Did he have a special technical skill? Was he handy? Did he have special knowledge of history or other subjects? What he proud, and how did he demonstrate that? How did he take care of the family home? What kind of work did he do or hobbies did he have?

You life story is not just about skills you have acquired to earn money. Think about your parents, your family and other intimate friends, and then note what you have learned from them as skills that could earn you money. Does the fact that you and your father used to do home improvement every summer apply to your retail business? Can you combine the fact that you know retail and home improvement to meet the needs of retailers in a particular way? It is always exciting to realize that you have an abundant number of possibilities for making money, feeling connected to your history and present, and understanding more about your true purpose.

TELL ME ABOUT YOURSELF

Many people mostly think about their business as "work."
There are two parts of the definition of work.

1. To exert oneself by doing mental or physical activity out of necessity.

2. To exert oneself by doing mental or physical activity for a purpose.

Some people start endeavors because they desire to "exert" themselves for a purpose such as expanding their skill set or to enjoy more of their life (if not all of it). However, most work out of necessity to earn a living in this world. Most people see money as the only necessity and all else is either not taken into account or granted very little attention. The result is you are a machine that works for money and has no purpose.

In your business, you must find a balance between the necessity to make money and your "purpose" for starting a business. As a new leader (or maybe a serial entrepreneur), this business is not just about your work history and resume. IT IS ABOUT YOU AND YOUR PURPOSE. Things that bring the most pleasure are those that you must list to start your business. If those things are not directly related to your business, PLEASE LIST THEM ANYWAY.

Within each of these activities are key skills. For example, you may like fishing. While your business is not about fishing, there are specific things you like about the activity. For example, you have to plan the trip (you like new information); you need to think deeply about the type of bait (you like to strategize), or that it is near nature (you like relaxed settings).

While earning money for the sake of earning money is very attractive, the less you enjoy your work, the less productive you are. Try understanding yourself from the inside out. List all the most practical and pleasurable things you truly enjoy doing. List all of the qualities about those things that you like. Look for the heart of those qualities that you enjoy.

IN SUMMARY

From all of this remembering, do lots of things fit together? How were some of the first people on your journey building block to live your life purpose? Can one or two or ten businesses be created from your life stories? As you connect the dots, know that you have lots of potential ways of creating products and services. For each purpose that you discover think about:

- What needs are you fulfilling in your business?

- What about your personal history explains the business, or businesses, that you're in and how you are most competitive in the market?

- What is it about you and your deep purpose that makes you best to manifest your business vision in reality? What do you do really well?

The term business, or creating to serve the needs and desires of others, is an amazing process. I hope you enjoy the dialogue with yourself to connect to infinite realities and possibilities.

⌒

Since the age of sixteen, CHENOA SMITH has started more than fifteen businesses in the media, advertising, entertainment, health, publishing and financial industries including being responsible for over $110 million in transactions, investments and media and technology applications. She is currently CEO of Living Theories Publishing www.livingtheories.com and has been in the business marketplace for thirteen years.

CHAPTER 27

The New Charm School©:

The Six-Figure Success Secrets of Gutsy Women

JENNIFER WARWICK, MA

HONEY, I DON'T CARE WHAT YOU'VE HEARD. The problem is not a glass ceiling.

It's a sticky floor.

Taking chances in our business lives is difficult for many women. We want to do things right or make the right choice. In fact, the biggest obstacle my clients wrestle with is insisting on being fully, deeply competent at something *before* taking it on. Women often seem to equate "competence" with "flawless performance," which is an unfairly high standard—and the stickiest floor of all.

In my work with Gutsy Women, many of whom are earning six-figures or more, I've found several common threads running through their stories. Linda LoRe, CEO of Frederick's of Hollywood, captured their philosophy in just six words:

Leap and the net will appear.

Of course, it's hard to leap when you're stuck.

So how do some women break free of perfectionism and other negative self-talk to become incredibly fulfilled and successful?

I've researched and listened carefully to the stories of dozens of Gutsy Women as diverse as Planned Parenthood CEO Mary-Jane Wagle, Pampered Chef founder Doris Christopher, former CNN executive Gail Evans, and many more. The lessons I learned laid the framework for my own business, The New Charm School, designed to help women succeed at work on their own terms.

Throw away the books on dressing for success. Toss that old copy of "Smart Cookies Don't Crumble." Forget about learning to play golf (the real deals are made in the locker room, anyway). And let go of your grandmother's idea of charm—sweet, deferential, lash-flutteringly proper.

Success in the new economy means teamwork, emotional intelligence, and interrelationships—skills at which women naturally excel. The New Charm School organizes the success secrets of six-figure women into nine easy lessons, each designed to help you break free of your current thinking and leap into a successful, fulfilling life.

BUBBLE BATH: TAKE TIME FOR CONTEMPLATION

If there were all the time in the world, my darlings, there'd be no one to buy six-minute abs and microwaves! Your life is already pretty full—especially if you are a woman running your own business—and taking time for yourself can seem self-indulgent.

It's not.

It's critical to take time to name your core values and develop a plan for your career. Suzanne DePasse, CEO (and, she notes, Empress) of DePasse Entertainment says, "Others can and will take advantage of you if you are not clear who you are and what you are building. Knowing your core values helps you chart a steady course and takes away the guesswork when making tough decisions. Build a business in line with your values and don't let trends blow you off course."

PEARLS: GO AHEAD, BE IRRITATING

Just as you can't get a gorgeous string of pearls without an irritant starting the process, your career and business success are sure to create some uneasiness on the way. Show yourself and those around you some compassion during the discomfort; stick it out and have faith that it will result in something extraordinary.

LIPSTICK: KNOW YOUR BOUNDARIES

Honestly, is there anything less attractive than a stylish, poised, successful woman with lipstick on her teeth? Correct application requires a steady hand, discipline, and a clear eye on the lip line.

To achieve success on your own terms, you need to know where your boundaries and limitations are and how to manage them effectively. Use 360-degree feedback, a mastermind group, a coach, a trusted virtual assistant or other tools to help you to identify your strengths (and delegate your weaknesses).

TIARA: OWN YOUR MAGNIFICENCE

A woman partner in a prestigious law firm shared that she couldn't understand why people seemed to dismiss her after meeting her at parties. After watching her introduce herself, the reason was clear. The male partners introduced themselves by saying, "I'm a partner in the Law Offices of X, Y, and Z."

She said, "Oh, I work with the X, Y and Z law firm." Her unwillingness to own her achievements was holding her back.

It's not enough to be great at what you do. Other people have to know, too. Show the stripes on your uniform; you've earned them.

SHOES, SHOES, SHOES: CHOOSE TO CHOOSE

Stilettos. Sneakers. Sandals. Marabou mules with a dainty French heel. They're all different—and they're all you. This trick is choosing what to wear and when.

Getting ahead in any business means weighing options, taking smart risks and making bold choices. Diane Reichenberger, CEO of Dualstar Entertainment Group (founded by very Gutsy Women Mary-Kate Olsen and Ashley Olsen), advises women to "build a foundation, find out what you're good at, stick with it, trust your gut…and then leave when it's right."

PAJAMAS: PLAY!

Gutsy Women know that life is too short to spend your time dreading the monotony of Monday mornings or being irritated by things unlikely to change. Consider Linda LoRe of Frederick's, an accomplished CEO who has taken an iconic company both into and out of Chapter 11.

At almost every presentation she makes, a man still raises his hand to ask, "Do you work with the models?"

"Oh, yes," she replies cheerfully. "I work with models morning, noon and night. Structural models, financial models, HR models, sales plan models…"

Go ahead—have fun and add lightness to your day.

CASHMERE: INCREDIBLY WARM, DECEPTIVELY LIGHTWEIGHT

Being successful does not mean being lonely. Six-figure women have exceedingly nurturing friendships. To them, having a strong support system is not up for negotiation. They achieve their goals—and then some—because they surround themselves with their secret weapon: others who will accept nothing less than their best work.

Make the most of your friends by asking and offering help whenever it's needed. Like cashmere, a circle of good friends is luxurious, comfy and well worth any investment. Why go it alone and insist on wearing rusty old chain mail instead? Trust me, sweetie; rust is not your color.

POCKETBOOK: GET WHAT YOU'RE WORTH

Let's face it. All the Suze Orman books in the world are not going to help if the fact is you are not making what you're worth in the first place.

Gutsy Women know that they deserve to be fairly compensated for their education, skills and experience—and they won't settle for less. Learn to negotiate for yourself, not just for other people. And don't make the same mistake Suzanne dePasse made when she became partners with her former mentor (or as she calls him, "tor-mentor") in their new multi-million dollar company. She was so flattered by the partnership, she says, that "I missed the part where he didn't put up any money."

CHAMPAGNE: BE OPEN TO POSSIBILITY

Where can you find inspiration and motivation? If you are willing to see it, it's everywhere.

When women's rights attorney Gloria Allred started her career, a mentor was hard to find, so she visualized the kind of lawyer women would want, and what a woman lawyer could be. The visualization was so powerful and effective that years later, when faced with a particularly vexing problem, she still finds herself wistfully thinking, "I wish I could call Gloria Allred."

Gutsy Women use the lessons of the New Charm School to spend their time looking forward, not at the ground. They focus on short-term wins that move them toward long-term goals; they have an appreciation for the impossible, the unexpected, and the mischievous. They see opportunities where others see too much work, and they see miracles where others see disasters.

And they're too busy leaping to ever get stuck to the floor.

JENNIFER WARWICK, MA is a women's career strategist, executive coach, writer and award-winning speaker. Her articles on management and leadership have appeared in numerous publications, and she is regularly quoted as a women's career expert in magazines ranging from Entrepreneur to Processor to Bombshell. Visit her daily blog, The New Charm School (www.jenniferinc.com/blog), or subscribe to her monthly e-zine at www.jenniferinc.com. To book Jennifer to present to your group, email veronica@jenniferinc.com or call (310) 695-7889.

PART III

SPIRITUAL FULFILLMENT

CHAPTER 28

Spirit's Words:
Believe in Yourself

YVETE BUGARINI

FROM TIME TO TIME, you—like me, probably get the sense that Spirit is talking to you. Or maybe you think you're just talking to yourself. Do you know what I mean? Sometimes the words come just after you directly request guidance, and sometimes they come out of nowhere. That's when I get all giddy inside. An idea will spark to create a product or a service, and I know it's from Spirit because I believe in Spirit's Words.

But, how do you know it's from Spirit? How do you know it's not "just you" thinking something quirky in your head...stop right there. Remove the feeling of "just you."

You are Spirit. Spirit lives within you.

I didn't realize at the time, but three years ago, I was about to embark on a journey of re-awakening. Over the course of time from 2003 until present day, I have made a conscious decision to finally hear what Spirit is telling me. Somewhere along the line, I realized that I was living in fear. I was suppressing the ideas and dreams that would truly make me happy because I didn't think I could "make" it happen. I was depriving myself from my own success. I didn't trust me.

Of course at the time I didn't realize I had this belief. I just knew that every time I had a great idea to create a product or service or to buy real estate…I would convince myself that I would never make it happen, and I would stop myself before I even started. I figured I would invest a ton of money into something, and it would flop, and I would be worse than before I'd started.

Perhaps you, too, have had an idea and then told yourself "Oh…it would never work" only to find out later, that someone else did believe in Spirit's Words and *did* turn the very same idea into reality? That's what I am talking about! Believe in Spirit. Don't mistake that good idea as nothing! Go for it.

When I started to "hear" the ideas Spirit was presenting to me, I began to ask myself some questions. So what if I just try? What is the worse thing that could happen? I could lose money. I wouldn't have a full-time job. I may fail and have to start over. But guess what? Spirit started to help me answer the questions: Would it really matter? Wouldn't there be people to help me up? Couldn't I pick myself up, dust off and start over? Hadn't I done that before? Would losing everything really matter? If I still had my faith and I believed in Spirit, wouldn't life be okay, no matter what?

I've always been a spiritual person and have always believed that I was pursuing God and my faith. But I never realized there is no "pursuit." I live and breathe Spirit's Words every day. Spirit is already within me. I don't have to worry about surviving or "making it." Spirit has my back!

Spirit has spoken to me several times over my lifetime, but I finally heard the words one day when I was journaling. I had an "automatic writing experience," and I just knew in my heart that I did not consciously write the words. For quite some time, I just talked about the experience.

Then, I realized the phrase even deeper. Spirit's Words. I wouldn't have received the message if it wasn't so. I realized I had some internal "work" to do! I posted affirmations. I recited the affirmation for the powerful woman, every morning. I went to NEW meetings and surrounded myself with like-minded individuals. I meditated and journaled (still do), and I began to focus my energy on being who it is Spirit wants me to be. Spirit wanted me to be anything I wanted to be! What? Wow, what a thrilling concept! I danced with glee—literally. I felt shivers all over.

I started believing in myself and what I heard. Then I decided to take one step at a time. I asked myself, what could I do to get the ball rolling? Before I knew it, I was creating a logo, writing teen books and taking classes that supported the vision. So far, Spirit has guided me, people have supported me, and whenever I ask, the resources appear. Day by day, the dream is developing into reality. Sometimes I don't know what the next step is, and sometimes I don't know where the money is going to come from, but I no longer worry about it. I get that Spirit is within me and is within you.

Have you ever heard people say that the Universe supports us? As I watch the miracles unfold with my path, I see that this is so true. The minute you commit to something of value, the Universe will make sure it happens. But you have to commit. You have to believe in what you are creating and focus your positive energy on the process.

"Life is not about finding yourself. Life is about creating yourself."

If you have a dream or get the nudge to try something out, go for it. One step at a time. Believe in yourself. Believe in Spirit. Trust the process and know that you can make it. Does all of this sound familiar? Do you hear this from successful businesswomen everywhere? Well, guess what? IT IS TRUE. Stop getting in your own way and make your dream a reality. Trust. Honor your Self. Honor where you are at in your process. Honor Spirit.

Over the last year I began breaking through the fear of this world, and I have committed to following my intuition to realize the life I am choosing to create. I know you can do it too! When an idea sparks in your head or tingles in your heart—that's Spirit. When you get all giddy inside about an idea—that's Spirit telling you that it's a good one. Don't mistake that. Embrace it. Commit to it and Don't Give Up—ever.

Many of us have been raised to be cautious. We are all responsible for our own prosperity, and sometimes we get confused by what that means. The fear of not being able to take care of one's self financially is a strong fear. Letting go of the idea that "I can't" or giving up the negative self-talk like…"What if I mess this one up…" is a process. Fear can paralyze us and fake us into believing that the dream is not possible. Letting Spirit's Words guide us is the ultimate freedom. Taking a chance on you is the most empowering experience. You might not know what's coming next, but if you trust in yourself and your intuition, Spirit can accomplish anything.

Begin by hearing Spirit's Words. Then, accept that it is all possible. Create your own powerful affirmations and set your intentions. Reaffirm them repeatedly. Take baby steps and watch yourself grow.

YVETE BUGARINI is CIO of Spirit's Words and 60/40. Every woman has the intuitive spirit, grace and power to be whomever she chooses. As a speaker, author and creator of affirmation products, Yvete has chosen to listen to Spirit, which has guided her to share with others how she discovered that Spirit's Words can change your life—if you just let them. Email Yvete at eveagle@hotmail.com or call (714) 538-5971 for speaking engagements or customizable affirmations.

CHAPTER 29

Five Simple Strategies for Awakening Your Soul

KATHY ESPER

WHEN CHRISTOPHER COLUMBUS SAILED TO THE NEW WORLD, most people believed the world was flat, and that he and his ships would fall off the edge of the earth. Christopher's belief and his journey proved that the world is not physically flat. The same holds true for our inner world. Our lives are meant to be full, rich and well-rounded. Yet, many people experience life as flat. They live in the Comfort Zone—a place that is safe yet doesn't allow them to experience life to the fullest.

At a recent lunch, my friend Lisa who is a highly successful entrepreneur said to me, "I don't know what my goals are any more. Money no longer motivates me. If I brought home $100,000 more a year, it wouldn't change my life."

Lisa's life is good. It's good and it's flat. Living in her Comfort Zone, she's craving growth and deeper fulfillment. She just isn't sure where to look for it anymore. It is from this place that our hearts and souls speak our deepest truths.

We know their language; however, often we're moving too fast to interpret their signals. Like Lisa, we recognize these signals, yet we aren't entirely sure what they mean. It follows that we don't know what to do to change our experience. We are left hanging and feeling "not quite right."

If this sounds familiar, know that you are not alone. Because we live in such a busy world, it's easy to retreat to our Comfort Zone where we miss opportunities. Usually we aren't consciously aware that we've missed anything, because we're so lost in going through the motions. But our hearts and souls always remind us of the truth. There is no questioning a heart tug.

YOU DON'T HAVE TO BREAK,
YOU JUST NEED TO BEND

Ours hearts and souls tend to speak loudest in areas where we have the greatest potential. Their messages point us in new directions that frequently require us to leave behind comforting beliefs and familiar ways. The prospect of leaving our Comfort Zone can be scary, especially because we are so good at convincing ourselves that if we step outside of our Comfort Zone, we will break. When really, we just need to bend.

Making small, simple shifts will help you to build the courage you need to move beyond your Comfort Zone and into the place where your soul feels fully alive—the place where you allow yourself to bend and grow in a new direction to become all you are meant to be.

FIVE SIMPLE STRATEGIES FOR AWAKENING YOUR SOUL

Awakening your soul is about developing complete trust in yourself and the Divine within you. It is a process that takes courage, patience and commitment. Aim to introduce one of these strategies into your life just two times this week. Next week, continue expanding in the way that feels best for you.

STRATEGY 1: PRACTICE THE ART OF STILLNESS

Spending consistent quiet time alone is the best way to reconnect to your heart and soul. It will re-sensitize you to your dreams and any area in which you need to grow. The signs are subtle, and you may not feel them right away. That's okay. Trust that they are there, and that you will feel them.

Achieving stillness in the midst of our busy and chaotic lives is surely a challenge. Start slowly. Wake up ten minutes earlier than usual and spend those ten minutes journaling or doing yoga. Or take a walk at lunch, breathe deeply, and pay attention to your breath. These actions will calm you down so you can hear your soul's messages more clearly.

STRATEGY 2: EXPRESS GRATITUDE

When you concentrate on what you are grateful for, you have a direct line into what matters most to you. Unimportant things fall away. Your perspective changes, and you begin attracting more people and experiences to be grateful for. It's as simple as like attracts like.

One terrific tool to develop this ability is a gratitude list. (This tool is fully explained by Sarah Ban Breathnach in her book *Simple Abundance*.) Each night before you go to bed, keep a journal of the ten people and things you are most grateful for today. You'll soon find that you're on a roll, and the list keeps growing! Creating this list is a lot of fun and often takes on a life of its own. Even when you've had a bad day, write ten things down. You will find that during the darkest times, your soul finds reasons to shine.

STRATEGY 3: SURROUND YOURSELF WITH SUPPORTIVE PEOPLE

One of the most important ways to distinguish between an ordinary and an extraordinary life is to create an outstanding support system for yourself. So often, we feel we have to do things on our own. Nothing could be further from reality. Just look at the team of friends and colleagues around any successful person you know. You can bet they surround themselves with people who are good for their soul, inspiring them to stretch their skills and build their courage.

Who in your life tells you the truth objectively, tells you things that no one else would dare to tell you, in a gentle way that will move you forward? Make it a point to spend time regularly with at least two people who inspire you to become the person your soul wants you to be. This one step will make the difference between ordinary and extraordinary success as you step out of your Comfort Zone.

STRATEGY 4: SHAKE UP YOUR ROUTINE

Remember that in every moment, change is happening. When something in your life feels monotonous, instead of accepting it at face value, stop and question why. Shake things up a bit. Order a different sandwich at lunchtime. Take an art class. Ride a horse on the beach at sunset. Do something simple that you've always wanted to do, or something you never thought you would do. Give yourself permission to explore your heart and rediscover your soul.

By asking questions, and choosing to make small changes in your routine, you'll send a message to yourself that you are strong enough to handle change. Any discomfort you have will be replaced with courage and confidence.

STRATEGY 5: FOCUS ON WHAT MATTERS

We get what we focus on. When we are living inside a Comfort Zone, our focus is probably just to get through the day. That is why a life lived in the Comfort Zone is a flat one. How clearly are you focused on what you truly want? Have you become so accustomed to multi-tasking that you've lost sight of what really matters to you? Or worse, you're doing so many things at once that life has become a blur.

To achieve a clear focus, you need to practice being completely where you are in any given moment. When you are in the middle of doing something, ask yourself if you are focused on the task at hand or if your attention is divided. Consciously focus your energy and fully experience each moment. By adding more focus into your day, peripheral things will fall away and you'll find yourself moving in the direction of your soul.

EMPOWER YOURSELF AND MAKE IT HAPPEN

Christopher Columbus courageously showed us that the world is not flat—physically.

Today's courageous souls are showing us that the world is not flat—spiritually.

Your greatest potential is beyond your wildest dreams. The Universe (God Force, Buddha, Jesus, the Divine, or whatever you choose to call it) is there to open doors as you travel your true path. You simply need to do your part and take consistent, focused action. By doing so, any part of your life that is flat will become more full and vibrant. Trust me, the results will be greater than you imagine.

KATHY ESPER is a passionate coach, actress and businesswoman. Kathy works with entrepreneurs, artists, and business professionals as they move beyond their comfort zones, follow their hearts, and hold their visions as more powerful than their histories. A member of the International Coach Federation, she has an MBA, over sixteen years of business experience, and a pure love for the arts. Contact Kathy at (508) 981-7106 or www.KathyEsper.com for individual and group coaching, speaking, and teleclasses.

CHAPTER 30

Manifesting your Inner Joy

ALLISON E. FRANCIS

"JOY" HAS BECOME AN OUTWARD EXPRESSION OF MY INNER SELF—an energy I send forth and receive back every day, in every healing way. I wear Joy like a silk shawl that warms my body, a comforting caress across my bare shoulders, or a loose, soft stroke across my soul. I hear Joy in my children's wild laughter as they canter on ponies in Griffith Park, in the chatter of water hens teaching their hatchlings how to bob for algae in the lake at Hampstead Heath, and in the twinkle of stardust and planet light circulating in the night sky above the shoreline in Hawaii Kai. Joy is everywhere.

But what is Joy? What is pure, unadulterated Joy? Is Joy a feeling or an experience? Is Joy a noun, a verb or an adjective? How might Joy be defined? According to the *Compact Oxford English Dictionary*, Joy is a noun that means "a feeling of great pleasure and happiness." Joy is derived from the Old French term *joie*—which in turn derives from the Latin word, *gaudere*, "to rejoice." We discover the verb "enjoy" means "to take pleasure in; (enjoy oneself) have a pleasant time." This term also originates from the Old French *enjoier* to "give Joy to." Perhaps we could say to "enjoy" someone or some event is to activate "Joy."

To engage in Joy is to en—Joy, or to enter into the Joy-filled state of life.

But we might ask ourselves, is Joy an easily identifiable term or an expression of being that is personal, subjective or mutable? Or is Joy a generic word applicable to any situation or feeling tone? Do we understand or recognize Joy when it occurs in our lives?

Joy is easily identifiable.

- Joy is a feeling tone.
- Joy is an experience.
- Joy is generic and personal.
- Joy is subjective and mutable.
- Joy is tangible and intangible.
- Joy is transient and transformative.
- Joy just is.

Joy is a term that most of us use to describe a concept, but rarely do we employ the word "Joy" in our daily lives to describe how we feel, what we experience, and how other people or moments affect us. We might say instead that we "love" this person or that object, or we are "happy" with a certain result we've achieved on a test, in a situation or in a relationship. Such loving, happy expressions are important; however, if we activate daily verbal expressions of how "joyful" or "joyous" we are through meditation and thanksgiving, we achieve a measure of inner peace and renewed Joy in our existence. Through the manifestation of this inner peace and joyful bliss, our lives become more centered, more creative and more enjoyable.

When we feel, experience or become Joy, we are allowing the free and full expression of our most natural emotional, personal and spiritual state—the state of pure love, pure happiness, pure bliss. Joy encompasses all of these feeling tones. When we vibrate on the Joy frequency, we are vibrating in the realm of the divine. When we vibrate as our most authentic, divine Self, other people are drawn into our loving, joyful energy. As we begin to share our Joy with others and they begin to share their Joy with us, we co-create a divine vibration in our mortal world.

By expecting Joy in all my personal, business and spiritual dealings, I encounter Joy on a daily basis. But to receive and give Joy, I create a climate within and outside myself where this joyful energy may flow freely. Meditation is a wonderful means of creating and maintaining a Joy-filled state of being. Although we sometimes think meditation must be a prolonged session that requires incense, a meditation CD, and specialized mats or meditation chairs, all we need is 15 minutes and a quiet space to tap into our Joy. I meditate in the early morning before my two children awake and our school day begins. I use this meditation technique every morning to tap into my inner Joy and to establish this self-affirming feeling tone for my day.

After you have found your quiet time and quiet space, find a comfortable position—either lying outstretched on a mat or your bed, or in a chair that supports your back. With your eyes closed, begin to breathe. Breathe in through your nose for 4-6 counts, then exhale through your mouth for 4-6 counts. Your ability to hold and release the breath will increase as this meditation becomes part of your daily practice. After you repeat these breaths for a few more counts, allow your body to soften and relax. Repeat this series until you have released any lingering tensions in your muscles, tendons, bones and psyche. Release the thought clutter in your mind and sink into the breath. Take your time; do not push yourself. Continue to breathe in this fashion until you are ready to feel your Joy.

When you feel ready, on the next inhalation, visualize "Peace." Let peace flow up from your toes and spread throughout your body, up through the top of your head. When you exhale, smile. Smiling relaxes your facial muscles and is a tangible manifestation of Joy. As you inhale again, visualize "Joy." Imagine Joy flowing to you from all corners of your room, your home, your neighborhood and the universe. Know that this Joy is eternal and infinite. It is the birthright of all living things. Now when you exhale, exhale "Joy." Allow your inner Joy to spread through your body and flow outwards, touching every aspect of your internal and external worlds. Continue repeating this series of peaceful and joyful breaths until Joy tingles and crackles within you, before expressing itself outwards.

Through these breaths, you are giving and receiving joyous energy, tapping into and manifesting your inner Joy.

When we are able to manifest Joy, to evoke our connectedness to Spirit, we rediscover that this intimate experience called life is always fluid, never static. Each day we should remind ourselves how Joy circles through moments in our existence—whether we move through a three-dimensional world or traverse multiple planes. And Joy, like Love and all things Good, Natural and Divine, is easily received, savored, and shared by us all—at all times!

Realizing and acknowledging the multi-faceted expressions of Joy connects us to all that is infinite and glorious in the universe.

Are not different joys Holy, eternal, infinite!
and each joy is a Love.
—WILLIAM BLAKE, *Vision of the Daughters of Albion*

ALLISON E. FRANCIS is an English professor at Chaminade University of Honolulu, a student of meditation, and a mother of two. Prior to moving to Hawaii, she taught at the American University in Baku and at the University of Leicester. Her fields of study include Vodou in Haiti; 19th century African American and Caribbean women's literature and hip hop culture. Allison co-founded Printed Mango Press (www.printed-mangopress.com), a small editing and publishing house in Honolulu.

CHAPTER 31

Expand Your Radiance— and Shine!

(In Your Life, Your Business, and the World)

JOYCE KENYON

"Remember Your Inner Sun Is Always Shining."
—BARBARA RAY, PH.D. Excerpt from *The Expanded Reference Manual of The Radiance Technique*® © 1985

HAVE YOU EVER WONDERED why some people who aren't brilliant or have a sparkling personality attract people to them like radiant magnets?

We all have a Seed of Radiance deep within us—a Cosmic Blueprint of Pure Spirit, Pure Light, and Unconditional Love—but few people ever fully ignite that Flame to illumine their lives and the lives of others.

Developing and expressing personal qualities of love, compassion and sincere interest in others will often attract others to you. Tapping into and amplifying your cosmic Inner Radiance is a powerful and different process.

However, just as our solar Sun is always shining (even on a cloudy day), clouds and fog can obscure it. Similarly, clouds of density can hide our radiance. In this chapter we will explore some human and cosmic ways to clear the skies and let our radiance shine.

STRESS CLOUDS OUR RADIANCE

Stress is an energy—neither positive nor negative—but how we perceive and react to stress (and how soon we do it) greatly affects our life. Mismanaged stress not only compromises our immune system and shuts down our creativity, memory and clarity, but when we're stressed, we actually repel people. Do you like to be with stressed-out people? They probably don't want to be around when you're stressed, either.

What can you do about it? The stress response is instant—and automatic. Nature has programmed us physically and psychologically to fight or run at the first sign of danger. You won't survive by negotiating with the tiger—or seeking a congenial relationship. In our modern-day jungle, relationships with your family, friends and clients can suffer because stress leads to fear, defensiveness and anger. The first step is to recognize your physical, emotional and/or mental reactions to stress. The next step is to dispel that stress-induced tension.

STRESS BUSTERS

In my Stress Mastery Seminars, I teach executives several Office Isometrics[sm] and One-Minute Meditations[sm], but here are two stress busters you can use anywhere. The key is to use them the moment you feel stressed.

1. Take a few deep breaths. It is impossible to maintain the same level of stress after taking a deep breath. Granted, some types of breaths are more useful than others, but any breath is better than none at all.

2. Tighten, then relax your neck and shoulders. Repeat this two or three times.

NURTURING YOUR OUTER RADIANCE

Radiance is a quality of Universal Energy, but it can express through your physical body, your emotions and your mind. Providing adequate nourishment for these can be a great support.

HEALTHY FOODS

It stands to reason that living foods are best for living people. Whether cooked or raw (preferably), find the kinds of foods that work best for your own body and lifestyle. As a general rule, high protein diets promote more activity, mental thought and/or aggression; more alkaline diets of vegetables, fruits and some grains tend to promote a quieter, more passive, contemplative state. Most importantly, don't be fanatic about it. Whatever you're eating, give it your loving attention and enjoy it.

THE AIR YOU BREATHE

Clean air can be hard to find these days, but quality air purifiers are available and living plants in your home and office provide beauty, added oxygen, and help to purify the air. Deep breaths not only relax you, but help to detox as well. Consciously fill your lungs with life-giving breath, then consciously exhale what you want to release.

THE IMPRESSIONS YOU RECEIVE

We aren't always surrounded with people who inspire us, but we can seek them out—in person or through books and tapes. Also, carefully select the TV shows you watch—and never fall asleep with the TV on, or it can negatively program you when you are most vulnerable.

ENLISTING YOUR UNCONSCIOUS MIND TO SUPPORT YOU IN ATTRACTING WHAT YOU WANT

You have already been programmed to get what you have— why not use the power of your unconscious mind to help get what you want?

Affirmations help you reprogram your psychological "computer." Here are a few tips: (1) Voice affirmations aloud three times each, with as much passion as you can muster. (2) Always use words that are wholly positive.; i.e. substitute "confident" or "courageous" for "unafraid." (3) Always state affirmations in the present tense— "I am"—not "I will be." Think of it as telling the truth in advance.

A good habit to make is saying affirmations—doing visualizations—or reading something that inspires you—as soon as you wake up in the morning and before you go to sleep at night.

LISTENING TO WHAT YOU'RE SAYING

We often reinforce our negativity with the words we use. Our negative words not only impact others, they affect us. We express our attitude with words, and our words, in turn, reinforce our attitude. You may think no one is listening to you—but your unconscious mind is always listening.

LOOKING FOR HUMOR, GRATITUDE & JOY

Laughter is powerful medicine, and we can use it often and without harmful side effects. It's also a great way to keep things in perspective. Gratitude is another blessing that enriches itself. Find and express your gratitude for small events like finding a parking spot, or the opportunity when stuck in traffic to take a deep breath, relax, and be glad you have a car to drive. Soon you may find that you are having gratitude for gratitude—and joy will follow close behind.

FINDING BALANCE—NOT BURNOUT

This has been a personal challenge for me because I love my work and could do it 24/7. Using a special technique, I also have a constant source of vitality and stamina. But I still need some exercise, at least five or six hours sleep at night, and an occasional change of pace. One thing I've discovered: we never *find* time to do things. We need to *make* time. Examine your own priorities and make time for them. A balanced life will enhance your radiance. No matter how successful you are in your work, fatigue or burn-out will dull your shine.

THE POWER OF MEDITATION

Most meditations will quiet your mind and body—and some give you valuable information and insight. A simple meditation is to sit quietly and watch your breathing. Don't analyze or try to change it. Just observe. Simply being present without thinking or doing anything is not so simple, but it can be learned.

There are also transcendental meditations such as TM® or using The Radiance Technique®, Authentic Reiki® which give you access to the Inner (not psychic) Planes of Soul and Spirit. These require special initiations by people capable of giving them, but they are profound in their ability to relax, transform and Enlighten us.

TRUE RADIANCE

Real (Inner) Radiance is a quality of Cosmic, Whole, Universal energy—and comes from the Inner Planes—the realms of Soul and Spirit. We can't fake it. We can't access or amplify it through our mind or emotions—but with the right tools, we can tap into and express that Radiant Power.

There are several transcendental practices (many of Eastern origin) that give us access to and use of these High Vibrations.

One of the best (and easiest) ways to promote Radiance and Healing on all levels (physical, emotional, mental, intuitional, Soul and Spirit) is The Radiance Technique®, Authentic Reiki®—also known as TRT®. Very different from what is commonly called "reiki," this is the original, carefully preserved and intact, Seven Degree Science that "Reiki" was originally. TRT® has no duality or polarity. It is not psychic energy or channeling.

This ancient, cosmic science not only gives us rapid stress release, effortless transcendental meditation, and a constant source of vitality, clarity, centeredness, and Radiance—it also provides direct contact with who we Really Are. With TRT® we are always able to powerfully and safely access, activate and amplify the vibration of Pure Light—Pure Spirit—the Whole of Existence— the Source of it All. It is the Light in Enlightenment.

Knowing what is in your human heart and in your Universal Heart—expanding your capacity for human love and for Unconditional Love—is an unending and joyous process. With TRT® you can also promote Radiant Healing, Harmony and Balance in yourself and every living thing you touch. And you can use it any place, any time and in any situation. I invite you to try it.

JOYCE KENYON is a Seventh Degree Initiate and world-known Authorized Instructor of The Radiance Technique® Authentic Reiki®. She produces and hosts the TV show "The Road to Health, Wealth & Higher Consciousness" and also teaches Stress Mastery Seminars to corporations and the public. For more than twenty years, her clients and students have included health care professionals, attorneys, entertainers, athletes and entrepreneurs. Joyce can be reached at (310) 285-3817, by email at RadiantJK@Radiant-HealingHands.com or visit www.Radiant-HealingHands.com.

⌒

CHAPTER 32

Universal Signs: The Real Path to Getting What You Want

MARCIA KING

DO SELF-HELP BOOKS THAT ASSUME YOU ALREADY KNOW WHAT YOU WANT FRUSTRATE YOU since all the premises for using their earthmoving principles start there? This used to frustrate me. The fact that I didn't know what I wanted frustrated me. How could I not know something so basic? I was smart. I wanted to be successful. I wanted the life of my dreams. I wanted…what?

Without that knowledge, and the clarity and focus that came with it, I was like a kid in the ice cream store, shifting from one foot to the next, stuck in a holding pattern. "Should I have strawberry, or vanilla, maybe pistachio or lemon sherbet?" Yet once I decided, a double scoop of Cookies and Cream on a waffle cone with sprinkles, and put my money on the counter, presto, it was handed over.

So what might be getting in the way of your decision? Here are some personal anecdotes, shared in encouragement. I hope they shed some light and lightness on the process.

"BE CAREFUL WHAT YOU WANT BECAUSE YOU JUST MIGHT GET IT..."

Sounds like you better know exactly what this monster looks like *before* you take any action, or you might regret your choice for all eternity. The snag is: how are you going to know if something really suits you unless you do 'get it'? Not getting it seems more dangerous to me. A beautiful dress in a shop window that's never tried on can become a false "ideal" against which real possibilities are measured...and discarded. This idealization can last a lifetime. Instead, try it on. Find out. How does it fit? What did you learn? It makes it easier to let go and try something else.

BUT I WAS SUPPOSED TO BE...

An illustrator, biologist, mother of five... Back in the late 1960's, I had the privilege of knowing Art Kane, a famous fashion photographer. He told me he had originally wanted to be an illustrator, but right out of school he was drafted into the Army and assigned to reconnaissance. His job was to take pictures. He discovered his photographer's eye and passion for the art. He let go of being an illustrator and loved his life in photography, and we have the gift of his photographs.

Stay in play. What you want will come to you, not necessarily in a linear way. In "The Artist's Way" Julia Cameron speaks to "doing the footwork." Go out and shake the apple tree...and be open when the Universe delivers oranges.

I'M NOT SURE. IT'S SUPPOSED TO LOOK LIKE...

I wanted a dog, specifically a black male German Shepard puppy so I volunteered for SPCALA. About two months later, a dog I hadn't walked or paid much attention to came up and put her paws in my lap. I noticed how thin she was. "No one is going to take her like this," I thought. "Maybe I could just take her home for a while and fatten her up." Her name is Comet, and I've had her almost five years now. She's not male, black or a puppy, but there is some Shepard in her. Amazingly, she was rescued on the exact day I decided to volunteer. She's an absolute joy, all I could want in a dog…and a reminder that what I want may not look the part, but it does show up.

I CAN'T ASK FOR…

This morning as Comet and I were walking in the hills I saw a man amongst some cactus crowned with prickly pears. "Hi," I said. "Are you collecting the fruit?" At first he seemed reticent, like he'd been caught with his hand in the cookie jar. "Would you like to try one?" he said. "Yes, I would." He picked one, took off a glove and got out his knife. First he cut off one end and then the other, exposing beautiful mango-colored flesh. Then he made two slits, removed a section of skin and held it out to me. As I reached over, he squeezed and the fruit popped into my hand. I'd always wondered what it would taste like. Now I know it's delicious.

HOW CAN I BELIEVE…

I got involved in coaching because I met a woman at the dog park, a life coach, and we became friends. I was struggling with what to do next with my life. I asked for a walk and a talk and got instead two coaching sessions that put me on this path. I remember standing in her driveway saying "Is it really this simple?" and she said, "Yes, just keep going and don't worry about how and when."

WHAT IF I COMMIT AND THERE'S SOMETHING BETTER…

Once you have something in mind, or something finally becomes real for you, go for it. Commit to it and then fasten your seatbelt.

The Universe can work instantaneously. On the last day of my Coaches Certification Program, I joined the International Coaches Federation and signed up/paid for a conference online. As I was typing in my credit card number I remember thinking "Okay God, guess I better have more clients to pay for all this." As the lid of my laptop snapped shut, the phone rang. It was a friend asking if she could hire me as a coach. Laughing I asked, "Sure, when do you want to start?" "How about now?" she said. Within the next three hours, the two random people I spoke to expressed an interest in being coached...and another friend called and asked to be a client.

DO YOU WANT WHAT YOU THINK YOU CAN GET OR WHAT YOU REALLY WANT...

Have you ever felt damaged beyond repair? I used to feel this. Since I've begun coaching, I've learned each of us come into this life with everything we need. All the elements are inherently here, undamaged. Unfortunately your own natural magnificence (and what you really want) can get covered over. But like a flea market table, when you sand off the crusty layers of old paint, do a little research to find the original hardware, and restore the finish, voila! There's the gracefully designed table you intuitively knew was there.

AM I THERE YET...

What you want doesn't arrive like the Queen Mary appearing one day in your harbor. It happens daily, monthly... every second. Each thought is a chance to get clear about who you are becoming and what you want. Little decisions are like baby steps. Do I paint my nails red or blue? Do I make my bed every morning? Do I tell the truth? Choose to become who you are, then do what you need to do, and see what shows up. What you want grows and changes with you. It defines who you are becoming.

THIS IS GOING NOWHERE...

Sometimes it feels like this. No movement. Yet we are moving. The Earth rotates and orbits, protons and neutrons are like mini galaxies, chakras spin, thoughts whirl. We are in motion, like concentric circles spiraling upward, a hawk gliding in an updraft; there will be times when you feel you're floating backwards instead of growing larger. It's just the backside of the curve. Don't fight it. Know you'll be on your way around. It's inevitable.

I'm still honing who I am, and the impact I want to have on this spectacular planet. It's like a wondrous sculpture being revealed. We do know what feels good for us. Risk that you might be right. Believe that God/The Universe/ You are creating and supporting the process on a daily basis, bringing in anything you want. Can you think of anything you want that's not available? I can't either.

MARCIA KING powerfully facilitates individuals to step into their most fulfilling lives. Her diversified background includes a BA in psychology from UCLA, worldwide travel, a successful career in sales and entrepreneurial venues, co-owning a custom home interior design store and writing literary fiction. She is a certified Co-Active Life Coach with Coaches Training Institute and a member of The International Coaching Federation. Contact: claritylifecoach@aol.com, phone at (310) 471-8703; subscribe to a FREE good-news newsletter@claritylifecoach. com.

CHAPTER 33

⌒

Birthing My Daughter, Birthing Myself

CHRISTINE KLOSER

HOW COULD THIS BE HAPPENING TO ME? Every plan I laid to have the "perfect" birth for my daughter was being ripped away, or so it felt. I had always been the type of woman who would set a goal, do my research, and forge forward to achieve whatever result I desired. I typically operated in the physical plane where I could will, force and "do" what I needed to experience success. What I learned from my daughter through the journey of birth broke me of this pattern. I finally "got it." I am not in control. There was a much greater force that knew my Divine Plan and knew my humanly ways needed an intervention.

But, why now? Why would I be robbed of the picture perfect birth I had planned for my daughter? By answering these questions for myself and discovering a deeper level of surrender, I hope it saves you some of the pain I experienced giving "birth" to my daughter... and myself.

It began when I had my annual gynecology exam. It just so happened this appointment had been scheduled for months, and it fell on the day after I took a home pregnancy test and found out I was pregnant. My husband and I couldn't be more excited and already felt the urge to provide only the best of everything for our child. Without even so much as a cheerful "congratulations," my doctor immediately performed an invasive vaginal ultrasound (I was not even four weeks pregnant) without an explanation as to why I needed it. She immediately sent me to have six vials of blood drawn for tests and asked me to set an appointment for another ultrasound in ten days. I would have set the appointment, but the receptionist who sat reading a tabloid gossip magazine was already "on her lunch break" at 11:59 AM, and she told me to call her later that day.

Everything about this doctor's visit felt wrong. So, I drove immediately to the bookstore to find some books about pregnancy that felt right. At first glance, I was disappointed at the number of books informing me about everything that could go wrong with pregnancy and childbirth. I distinctly remember quickly putting those books back on the shelf. Thankfully something called me to keep looking for books that weren't based in fear, but instead were based on the belief that my female body was born to birth. I was designed to carry my child and birth him/her as naturally as I could. Yes, that felt right. And, after much searching I found a few books that spoke directly to my heart and how I felt about the perfection of my pregnancy.

I never called that doctor again or had any additional unnecessary tests. Through a friend of a friend, I was introduced to an incredible doula and talented midwife who shared alternative birthing options with us. We chose a home birth. Yep! We wanted what we considered the gentlest birth possible for our daughter, so we chose to birth at home in water with the assistance of an experienced midwife and doula. This was definitely right.

I was in heaven watching my belly grow, feeling the first kicks and wearing maternity clothes. I took great care of myself through diet, exercise, rest and asking for a lot of help especially with my business. When people asked if I was nervous about home birthing, I confidently said "No." We had done our research, had one of the best back-up gynecologists in Los Angeles, had a back-up plan in case anything happened at any stage of pregnancy or birth, and I was a perfect candidate for a low-risk birth. The more I learned, I realized I was more scared about birthing in a hospital than I was at home. My plan was unfolding perfectly, and I felt more and more like a female goddess, connected with the generations of women before me who birthed in fields, yurts, and most importantly amongst other women. Then, everything changed.

My midwife commented that she felt a hard spot both under my ribs and in my pelvis and couldn't exactly distinguish which was the head and which was the bottom. She suggested I go to my back-up doctor for an ultrasound to confirm the baby's position. At that time we would have to decide if we would do something as invasive as an external cephalic version if the baby were breech. That's when they manually turn the baby to a head down position so the mother can deliver vaginally. My husband and I went back and forth about whether or not we would do this. We felt if our baby was meant to turn, it would on its own. Who were we to make that decision for our unborn child?

We soon learned no decisions needed to be made. The doctor discovered our baby was breech, and she couldn't be turned for three reasons. She was frank breech, the hardest breech to turn. My amniotic fluid was low, and my placenta was on top of my belly and could be ruptured during such an invasive procedure. With one look at the ultrasound, I felt every plan I had ever made had been destroyed. How could this happen to me? I was the picture of health! I had done everything right and always achieved the goals I set forth. No, this wasn't going to happen to my baby and me. I knew there had to be something I could do.

I did it all. I researched every possible way to get my baby to turn. I figured I could "do" this, too. I went to the acupuncturist, chiropractor, intuitive healer and homeopath. I laid on an inversion table several times a day, talked to my baby, cried a lot and listened to the "How to Turn Your Breech Baby" CD. My life had become about turning my baby. The loss of my perfect birth plan had triggered something deep within me that was scared of losing control. I felt I was mourning the loss of having my ideal birth, and the feeling of control I had over my life. The experience of realizing God was in control was both gut wrenchingly painful and incredibly freeing.

In the midst of all of this emotional turmoil, our doctor and doula suggested we schedule a Caesarean birth. Again, we asked ourselves, "Who were we to determine our baby's birth date? Shouldn't our baby decide when she's ready to come into the world?" We soon learned that birthing a breech baby as an emergency procedure could be traumatic, and if we scheduled the Caesarean birth, I wouldn't be treated as an emergency patient. We chose to schedule the procedure so the doctors and nurses would be more able to provide a gentle entry for our little angel. But, still I didn't stop lying on the inversion table and praying for my baby to turn.

When we scheduled the birth for February 15, 2005, we also decided to go to Ojai, CA to celebrate Valentine's Day and prepare ourselves to welcome our child. By this point, I had begun to let go of my "plan" and trusted the perfection of this experience and wisdom that my baby knew what she was doing. Suddenly and certainly, I felt more prepared to be a mother, having realized how little control I have. My faith in God and His Divine plan was getting stronger by the moment, and I knew the most important thing was for our baby and me to be well taken care of through the actual birthing process.

February 12th arrived. The final baby shopping was done. I had friends scheduled to deliver meals and diapers. I turned business over to my assistant, and we were completely ready for the scheduled birth. We even found time to enjoy a Valentine's dinner party with friends. An hour into the party, my water broke! We were an hour away from home, 90 minutes away from the hospital and without our hospital bags!

As fate would have it, our doula had just gotten home from a 36-hour birth, our doctor was willing to drive 90 minutes on his off-duty Saturday night to birth our child, and we had time to drive home and pack our bags. By 11:15 PM we had all converged at the hospital. Our doula photographed the entire birth, the doctor let us play music from Spa Ojai (the next best thing to being there), and we became the proud parents of a beautiful baby girl at 12:48 AM on February 13, 2005.

Yes, I still have a very noticeable scar from the Caesarean, and my healing process was rather intense, but every time my daughter flashes her big gummy smile, I'm reminded of the gifts she gave me through her birth. I learned to trust her, trust my Divine Plan, be authentic in sharing my fears, let go, surrender to what is, and above all to have an undying faith that everything happens for a reason.

As you journey through the ups and downs, joys and challenges, fears and faith, remember there is a Divine plan working through you. There are gifts in the experience at hand, and the quickest way to receive them is to let go and trust Divine order. All is well, right now. Yes, I birthed our beautiful daughter, and she also birthed me… as the woman I always yearned to be. Thank you baby Janet Rose and thank you God.

CHRISTINE KLOSER is the president of Love Your Life Publishing and the founder of NEW Entrepreneurs, Inc. She helps entrepreneurs and experts become published authors. She is featured in Starting Your Own Business, Heart of a Woman and Secrets of the Millionaire Mind. She has been a guest on numerous local/national radio and TV shows, and her quotes appear in a variety of publications including Entrepreneur Magazine, Palisadian Post, Argonaut and Woman's Day. Contact Christine at (310) 962-4710 publish@loveyourlife.com, www.LoveYourLife.com www.NEWentrepreneurs.com.

⌒

CHAPTER 34

Your Higher Self
Is Just a Color Away!

Experience a Lighter Brighter You with Color Therapy

CONSTANCE HART

I'M A PASSIONATE CERTIFIED COLOR THERAPIST and am often asked, "How did you get into color therapy? It's so very unique." For a while it was difficult for me to answer this question since my journey has included many twists and turns, but one day I simply realized: I'm a daughter of artists, and I grew up in a home surrounded by color. This has clearly had an effect on my exploration of color psychology.

In fact growing up, our living room wall and even our furniture was painted with flowing rainbow-colored waves. My bedroom had bright red wallpaper and multi-colored patchwork carpeting. There were colorful pillows everywhere and an abundance of art supplies. Spending time in our home meant being inundated with color. Now I fully appreciate my upbringing, as I have naturally understood color as a force that has positive effects on our body, mind, emotions and spirit.

COLOR IS ENERGY

Color is an invaluable tool we have to enhance our life experience. Scientists have revealed that we humans are more than just physical matter—we are energy, and colors are the waves of energy that we can actually see. This makes color an easily accessible energy source you can call upon to realign and balance your inner self. Each color has a distinct vibration that mirrors various energy frequencies in your being; thus they act like a magnet to bring internal harmony.

If you're interested in realigning, balancing and/or elevating your energy, exposure to a particular color or color combination will successfully create a shift.

Learning how each color frequency affects you physically, mentally and emotionally allows you to expand your energy balancing "tool kit" to feel lighter and brighter on all levels. As you discover where you are energetically deficient, you can consciously call upon the external frequencies of color to affect your internal energy. Of course there are intricacies to personalized color therapy, but the general guide that follows will help you get started in expanding your awareness to the greater benefits of color energy.

YOUR INNER ENERGY CENTERS

You have seven major energy centers in your being. These are called Chakras (true Sanskrit pronunciation is "cha" like "cha cha cha") as defined by the ancient philosophy of yoga. The word Chakra means "wheel," to denote a spinning wheel of energy. These seven energy wheels are a blueprint to your entire life experience—for each Chakra not only governs particular organs and glands but also unique mental and emotional qualities, demonstrating the interconnectedness of your body, mind and spirit.

Each Chakra can be activated by exposure to one of the seven colors of the rainbow. Because each rainbow color is a refracted portion of pure white light, as you begin to play with your color therapy awareness, you'll be reminded that you are inherently a light being or as I was trained—a "hue man" (hue meaning "light" and man meaning "being")!

When your Chakras are blocked, you hold stagnant un-vibrant energy in your physical and ethereal bodies. In the energetic world of healing, we believe this to be the root cause of disease. Stagnant energy flow blocks your optimal health as well as your mental capabilities. When your Chakras are clear, unblocked and awakened, energy flows throughout your being, sourcing your organs and glands successfully with vibrant energy while enlivening your mental capacity, emotions and spiritual experience.

COLOR ENERGY GUIDE

With conscious exposure to color energy, you can increase the flow of energy throughout your energetic system and experience better health as well as the truth of who you are—balanced light energy. Here's a starter guide to the seven rainbow rays and their general metaphysical benefits. Other color frequencies exist that are blends of these rays, and those colors have distinct energy benefits as well.

RED—specific benefit to the Root Chakra- your energetic base, which governs the lower body from the perineum downward for healthy functioning of the colon, adrenal glands, the male sex organs and the strength of your bones. Awakens life force, active, determined and passionate energy as well as a sense of stability and grounding.

ORANGE—specific benefit to the Sacral Chakra- your emotional center, which governs the lower belly to lower back for healthy functioning of your kidneys, bladder and the female reproductive organs. Awakens creativity, sensuality, feelings, emotions, patience and a nurturing mothering energy.

YELLOW—specific benefit to the Solar Plexus Chakra- your will center, which governs the mid section of the body for healthy functioning of your digestive organs, the liver, gallbladder, pancreas and spleen. Stimulates clarity, focus, self-esteem, self-confidence, releasing fears, doubts and confusion.

GREEN—specific benefit to the Heart Chakra- your balance center, which governs the upper chest to upper back for healthy functioning of the heart muscle, respiratory and circulatory system. Awakens unconditional love, generosity, internal balance between active self and inward reflective self, healthy boundaries and relationships.

BLUE—specific benefit to the Throat Chakra- your purification center, which governs the shoulders, throat, trachea, jaw, mouth, teeth, gums, nostrils and ears. Stimulates total purification of senses, effective peaceful communication, and an overall sense of calm.

ROYAL BLUE—specific benefit to the Inner Eye Chakra—your awareness and perception center, which governs the sinuses, external eyes, pituitary gland and partial brain space for balance of the brain and awakening of your intuition. Awakens psychic abilities and a deep sense of trust.

VIOLET—specific benefit to the Crown Chakra, which governs the pineal gland, partial brain space and top of head for synergy of all glands and an opening to energy that lives outside the physical body. Stimulates higher reason and purpose, spirituality and meditative self.

When you are off-balance you will tend to have blocks with coordinating colors, meaning a particular color will not elicit the above-mentioned benefits. This is where personalized color therapy is helpful, as other color energies can be utilized to open up blocks in rainbow color sensing and experiencing. I spend time "getting into" my clients' eyes to discover first how an individual is responding to each Chakra color. Then I bridge any gaps with what I call the Conscious Colors®—the colors that lie in between each Chakra color.

I encourage you to play with the rainbow colors and find your own personal associations and responses.

PROFOUND SHIFTS CREATED SIMPLY

There are several simple ways to successfully "play" with color as a means to enhancing your physical energy, nourishing the health of your organs and glands, stimulating your ability to be focused, clear, productive and creative, as well as reducing stress and creating more balance in your daily life.

Here are a few suggestions:

- Gaze intently and meditate with needed color energies
- Wear clothing of specific energy colors
- Sleep on solid-colored sheets
- Use colored bathroom towels
- Brush with a "color energy" toothbrush
- Drink out of a colored mug or glass
- Eat off a colored placement

- Surround yourself with colored paper, pens and folders
- Put a color energy desktop on your computer screen
- Use a colored entry mat for your home

Let your intuition be a guide and as you practice trusting your intuition, you'll receive the added benefit of balancing your brain space!

Your mind is very powerful, so as you gaze at color with 1) the conscious awareness of what each color vibration has to offer your inner being and 2) the decision that colors create an energetic shift in your being, your brain sends a message, like a ripple effect, through your nervous system. New energy in the form of thoughts and color frequencies take shape.

Color energy therapy is a most enjoyable means of connecting to the Higher Self due to its positive approach and active affirming nature. I encourage you to discover the light of color today!

CONSTANCE HART owns Conscious Colors® and is a nationally recognized color therapist and Chakra expert. She's a visionary in the field of color psychology and a pioneer with color aromatherapy with her line Color Aromas™. Constance is in high demand as a spokesperson/expert and presents workshops and classes. Visit www.consciouscolors.com to receive your FREE newsletter or order a Comprehensive Chakra Guide. Schedule a consultation or distance healing by emailing constance@consciouscolors.com or call (805) 305-0046.

CHAPTER 35

Living Your Soul Print

KIM MITCHELL

WHILE ON THE PHONE WITH A BUSINESS CONTACT, a voice told me to ask if she knew anything about getting speaking engagements on cruise ships. This was in the midst of a discussion on setting up workshops for motivational speakers. The question that I was being urged to ask did not appear to fit the context of the conversation. Even though the idea of speaking on cruise ships had been on my mind for over a month, I argued with my voice.

I have learned, sometimes through suffering, to surrender to that little voice. I asked the question. She had all of the information I needed. Less than one week later, I was booked to provide workshops on two seven-day cruises. By the end of the year, I booked four cruises and presented at two health resorts. I was in the flow of the Universe, and everything was coming with such ease and grace that I could hardly believe it was happening. Things could not have been easier.

How do we arrive and remain in that place where we live in the flow of the Universe? How do we accept what our souls are calling us to do with the extraordinary lives we have been given?

We have to embrace what Rabbi Mark Gafni calls our soul print. Soul print is synonymous with your mission or life purpose. It is what you are here to do and to bring to the world. All of us have a reason to be here, and it is part of our life journey to discover what it is and to share it. Our soul print is what makes each of us unique. It is the special talents and gifts that we have and express in a way that no one else can.

God, the Universe, or whatever name we know as our Supreme Being needs us. We are God's arms and legs. When we express our unique gifts, we show all that God is. We are expressions of God in this world. This means our soul print is important to share because if we don't share it, the world does not get it. Yes, we absolutely need God! Yet, God needs us as well.

ACCESSING JOY

When we observe someone else is sharing his/her unique soul print, and we know that we are not sharing ours, we become jealous. This is why we sometimes feel jealous of our friends when something good is happening for them. Success is in limitless supply, yet we see it as limited when it isn't appearing in our lives. If we are living our soul print, jealousy is eradicated. We are all one; one person's success is also my success.

Yet success is not as strong a motivational tool as we would sometimes believe. As human beings, we are driven by the need to connect with other people more than we are driven by success. We use various means to get that feeling, but connection is what we ultimately seek. We need to know our oneness and union with God through our connection with others. Many of us do not acknowledge this need. Like Sigmund Freud, we think that physical contact will make us feel connected to one another. Then we wonder why we often feel lonely, even when physical contact with others is attainable and consistent.

Why are we so often lonely if connection is our greatest drive or need? Loneliness is the result of the inability to share our soul print with others. When we cannot share, we feel isolated. Those who have the opportunity to share their unique gifts with others feel more connected. This is why we experience so much joy when we volunteer to help others, even though we perceive the receivers of our efforts as the beneficiaries. It is not the physical contact that makes us feel joy. It is sharing our soul print that gives us the feeling of connection to something larger than ourselves.

As individuals, we have all been given the right to the pursuit of happiness, yet pursuing happiness has not brought us joy. In most of our lives, joy is like a butterfly that sits quietly on our shoulder only when it is not being chased by a butterfly net! Passionately pursuing our soul print allows us to access joy. Joy is a by-product of living and sharing our soul print.

FIVE STEPS TO LIVING YOUR SOUL PRINT

Many of us are completely unaware of what our soul print is. We spend so much time working to make ends meet, pursuing pleasure, and warding off pain that we do not take the time to find out our mission or life purpose.

These five steps will help us to accept the unique invitation of our lives—our soul print.

1) Listen. That little voice in our minds is the voice of God speaking or intuition. Whatever name we assign to it, this voice is powerful and purposeful. Pay attention to this voice.

   In addition, our bodies speak to us and can assist us in discerning what works in our lives. Take the time to slow down and pay attention to how your body responds to certain activities. When we are pursuing passions that are right for us, we often feel better physically. When we pursue things that are wrong for us or agree to things that we don't really want to do, we often feel uncomfortable physical sensations or pain.

2) Pursue your soul print. Once we have listened and we know what our soul print is, we should passionately pursue it. Rather than claiming our right to pursue happiness, let us claim our right to live joyfully. Joy is a by-product of living your story or your soul print.

3) Be receptive. Being receptive is just as important as pursuing your goals. When you are living your soul print, unexpected opportunities will come to you as a result of the consciousness you are claiming. Be open and receptive to these opportunities, even if they involve activities in which you never imagined yourself participating. Remember: things that are alike tend to attract one another. You are an abundant, soul-satisfied person; therefore, abundant, soul-satisfying opportunities are drawn to you.

4) Give it away. Anything we don't think we have enough of we can usually afford to share. By sharing we show the Universe that we are willing participants in the circulation of good. Oftentimes we feel that if we are not financially compensated for our work, it is not worth the time to share our unique gifts. The truth is, we cannot out-give God no matter how hard we try. How many times have we given our time to charity or to a cause and found that we benefit spiritually as much, if not more, than the person or organization to whose aid we have come?

5) Declare your intention. Loneliness is the result of an inability to share your soul print. We are driven, as humans, to connect with others. Tell people what you hope to accomplish in sharing

your gifts. Put it in their minds so that the consciousness of "two or more gathered" can go to work on your behalf. Allow that connection with others to fuel your intent.

Share your soul print!

KIM MITCHELL is a graduate of Stanford University and a proud LA native. She earned an MFA in film directing and a Masters degree in education from UCLA. Mitchell's film projects have garnered awards including a Motion Picture Association of America Award and the Lynn Weston Fellowship. Kimestry Arts Network is Mitchell's entrepreneurial venture including speaking, staff development and creative playshops. Clients can visit kimestryarts.com or call (310) 338-9756 and attend the next playshop free. Kimestry inspires, supports, and facilitates creative people in experiencing community, wholeness, and creative freedom.

⌒

CHAPTER 36

How to Transform Childhood Wounds by Raising Your Energetic Vibration

DIANE PETRELLA, MSW, CPCC

CHILDHOOD ABUSE, NEGLECT AND PSYCHOLOGICAL TRAUMA leave profound emotional wounds rooted in guilt, shame and self-hatred. This pain carries a matching energetic vibration that is encoded in your psyche, body and belief system. These low energy vibrations weaken your ability to easily move forward in life and create resistance to having the life you desire.

We carry within thoughts and feelings stemming from emotionally charged childhood experiences. These thoughts and feelings form our belief system in adulthood. Your inner reality and its associated energetic vibration match your outer reality and the vibration of the experiences you attract into your life. If you have a core inner belief of negative self-worth, the energetic frequency of that belief, like a magnet, draws forth disappointing and stressful experiences that match the vibration of negative self-worth. By raising your energetic vibration and shifting your thoughts and feelings, you attract higher-level experiences resulting in greater peace and inner joy. This chapter offers you strategies designed to raise your energetic vibration and open new pathways to higher level emotions and experiences of joy, acceptance and self-love.

MY PERSONAL TRAUMA

He died instantly. My father fell down the cellar stairs and was gone. I saw the whole thing. I still recall vividly the clamoring tumble of his body falling, seeing him lie lifeless on the cold cement floor, hearing the piercing sirens of the police rescue, and with numbing horror, feeling the blood stains on my blue chenille bathrobe. Only eleven years old, my life as I knew it vanished. On that fateful October evening, I was catapulted out of my childhood into a world of grief and despair that lasted nearly two decades.

I am forever grateful that, at the age of twenty-nine, I found a masterful therapist who introduced me to the world of spirit and connection with my higher self. As a traditionally trained therapist, I knew how the process worked. But Lee was amazing. He opened me to a world I always knew existed but never knew how to access. Integrating spirituality within traditional healing work accelerated my growth enormously.

Through my personal healing journey and the work I do as a therapist and life coach, I offer you three simple yet life transforming strategies to assist you in your growth and personal evolution. May you, too, experience the wondrous healing powers of the Universe.

THE POWER OF GRATITUDE

Experiencing appreciation and gratitude are key emotional states fundamental to raising your energetic vibration. Research on the power of gratitude shows that grateful and appreciative people take better care of themselves, are more optimistic, and are more motivated about attaining life goals.

What does this mean for you? Keep a daily gratitude journal.

Start each morning or end each day by thanking the universe for the gifts offered. I've kept a gratitude journal for years and can feel my energy lift as I write. Thank the Universe for the bright sunny day you had, for lunch with a close friend or for the cold that reminded you to slow down your pace. These are all the simple things we often take for granted but which create the fabric of our life. When we thank the Universe, we open a pathway to receive more. Think of when you give something to someone and they don't acknowledge or thank you for your gesture. Do you want to keep giving to that person? Now think of someone who is appreciative and grateful. You want to give more to that person. It's the same with the Universe. Lack of appreciation and gratitude is like turning your back on a loving, giving friend. Your gratefulness opens the door to receive more.

If you are currently dealing with a great deal of pain, keep a more traditional writing journal to release your thoughts and feelings. On a cellular level, writing produces a physiological release and helps remove traumatic memories stored within your body. And emotionally it helps provide some ease of distance from your pain.

You accelerate your healing by combining traditional writing for release with keeping a gratitude journal. The higher-level vibration of thankfulness serves to gently minimize the lower energies of your pain and sadness. By doing this you allow the gifts in your life to become a comforting blanket you wrap around your pain.

CARE OF YOUR BODY

There is a direct link between how we care for our bodies and how we feel about ourselves.

If you were physically or sexually abused as a child, your body was the receptacle for the abuse you endured. This may have engendered feelings of self-hatred and a sense of anger, disregard or even contempt for your body. These feelings may be reflected in how you take care of yourself. One strategy to help you improve your self-esteem, lift your energetic vibration and develop a greater sense of self-love is to protect, nurture and care for your body. Think of your body as your best friend who needs your love and attention.

How is your nutrition? Do you exercise? Do you keep preventive medical appointments? Do you pamper yourself? Choose one thing to do that is nurturing to your body. Perhaps you intend to drink eight glasses of water daily for one month. Or perhaps you will decide to walk fifteen minutes three times a week or to have a weekly massage. As a long-time runner one goal I set for myself was to run a marathon every decade. As I reach my fiftieth year I am training for my fourth marathon. It is my commitment to me and my body and a reflection of the gratitude I feel for my health.

Choose something that is healthy, medically necessary, relaxing or soothing. Stretch yourself a bit yet be realistic about what you will accomplish. Stick with it for at least one month and notice what changes occur emotionally. Once that becomes a habit, add something else.

Be aware of what you say to yourself because your intention behind your action is as energetically important as the action itself. Choose compassionate, respectful and loving thoughts while keeping promises to yourself. For example, by saying, "I really don't want to walk tonight" you are sabotaging yourself and diminishing the positive effects of your walk. Train your mind to stay positive and committed by saying, "I feel tired, but it is important for me to take good care of my body; I'll feel great afterwards," or "I feel so healthy when I drink this water." These loving thoughts and nurturing actions lift your energetic vibration and open a pathway towards greater self-love and personal fulfillment.

DE-CLUTTER YOUR CHILDHOOD MEMORY PATH

Everything is vibration—including the objects with which we surround ourselves. An extremely powerful healing strategy is to discard anything in your environment that diminishes your energetic state. By eliminating objects that symbolize sadness and disappointment, you energetically clean house and set the intention to move away from your pain towards a path of fulfillment.

When I learned of the power of de-cluttering, I planned a ritual for myself. I burned in my fireplace years of journals filled with painful feelings and stories of unfulfilling and disappointing relationships. One of the emotional consequences of the early traumatic loss of my father was my tendency to connect with unavailable men. I was filled with so much grief, sadness and fear of abandonment that I kept manifesting relationships fraught with grief, sadness and abandonment. I kept repeating the pattern because that was the level at which I was vibrating. After I burned these journals and purged myself of many other objects I felt an immediate sense of spiritual openness and lightness. Within four months I met the love of my life. Coincidence? I hardly think so.

What are you holding onto that no longer serves you? What do you have in your environment that no longer is meaningful? What energies of pain and sadness still linger in your living space? Make a commitment to start with one thing and let it go. By doing so, you energetically release yourself from the prison of your past and become open to the abundance you deserve.

⌒‿⌒

DIANE PETRELLA, MSW, CPCC is a psychotherapist and certified life coach. She co-founded the first child sexual abuse treatment program in Rhode Island and has been working with individuals and groups for over twenty years. Specializing in psychological trauma, her coaching business is designed to teach individuals the inner spiritual technologies of energy, thought and intention to create transformational, lasting change. Contact Diane at (401) 831-1341 or diane@newpathwayscoaching.com Subscribe to her free monthly newsletter at www.newpathwayscoaching.com.

CHAPTER 37

The Gift of Intuition

RUTH SANCHEZ

EMOTION AND A LITTLE GNAWING FEELING inside my stomach sometimes rule intuition.

Intuition has caused me to act and react until I felt I was on the right path.

WHAT IS INTUITION?

Henri Bergson, a French philosopher stated his belief that intuition is a surer guide than scientific analysis to the understanding of reality and truth. Through intuition, Bergson believed, man discovers the Universe to be a process of duration, the expression of an elan vital (life impulse)—that is the creative force of nature. (New standard encyclopedia)

Or in my simple English: Intuition is the opposite of scientific. It is what cannot be explained.

It is what we feel, what we think, and the reason why we do corny things sometimes. Intuition makes us act reasonable and unreasonable. It's why we love more and for reasons that make no sense to anyone else. And also what a mother feels when her child has been injured and knows it instantly.

Ever been able to finish someone's thoughts? Finish their sentences? Did you know you were going to get THAT phone call? Did you have a thought or a vision in your mind's eye and it came true? Could you tell the sex of a baby before it was born? How about the phone call that made your stomach turn before you picked up the phone? These are examples of using your intuition.

Does this mean you are gifted? Does this mean you have a special talent? What it does mean is you have a gift. You have a talent. You are gifted when you use it, and talented when you grow it. Yes, you get better when you honor what gifts and talents you already have.

Here are some exercises you can do on a daily basis to help grow your gift:

- Guess who is on the phone calling you before picking up the phone.
- Guess what is going to happen in the show or movie before it happens
- Guess who is at your door when the doorbell rings.

Some ways to listen to your intuition better are:

- Relax: be comfortable and think freely. Take it simple and go easy.
- Think in simple terms; in colors and shapes.

Intuition is usually spontaneous, like thoughts that seem to just pop into your head.

Intuition is basically a simple process of understanding that words, pictures, sounds, and movies in the mind are the way your spirit is communicating with you so you will understand.

Certainly there can be confusion, it comes with the territory. As you work with your intuition and interpret messages you receive, your messages become more and more clear.

Put preconceived notions aside, and then the real intuitions can come through less clouded.

Think less, feel more.

Intuition deals more with feelings and emotion, while thinking deals more with rational thoughts. Thoughts come from the head, and feelings come from the heart.

Very often there will be conflict between the head and the heart or thoughts and feelings.

When a major decision is on the line, follow the heart. The heart will better lead you to your path of destiny, and your heart's desire.

While thinking is good, paying attention to feelings is more accurate. Thinking is what we already know to be scientific, and it can start an internal argument between the head and the heart.

Do you recall what your teachers said while taking a test? They recommend going with the first answer that pops into your head. Why? Our brains recall what is best first. Our bodies love emotional highs. When we get a right answer, we feel great! We are encouraged to do it again.

If you ever go to a psychic, make sure they are not tiny; make sure they are a medium, or a large. (H a Ha!)

DREAMS

Dreams have meaning. If your doctor or therapist asks, "How are your dreams?" And you say, "I am having nightmares." The doctor says, "That is good. You are letting off steam behind sleep." There are messages in dreams that we do not always recognize in a conscious state. Daydreams are goals. Intuition helps to achieve these goals.

It is my belief that God intended for life to be enjoyed and for it to be pleasurable.

Life does take work and after work comes the reward. Intuition is available to help us get to our life's path and get our life's dreams. When I listened to my head, life became confusing, and the same experiences happened repeatedly until I became clear and focused and then began to listen to my heart.

Oprah calls this listening to the whisper. If I do not listen to the whisper, the bricks start falling on my head. This means that life starts getting difficult in that particular area until I learn my lesson. There are times when I can be stubborn and keep listening to my head, then I end up beating up my heart. In the end my heart will win. I am learning to listen to the whispers early on because frankly, being hit spiritually by a truck really hurts.

Part of feelings is love. The most important place for me to be is in love. Working from a place of love is where most of my creativity and freedom come from. The greatest feeling is being in love and being loved in return. When this occurs, the heart will usually draw you to your path with feelings of anticipation versus anxiety.

During my journey to achieving my path, there are four things I attribute to growing my intuition: chances, changes, choices and challenges. Would I change anything? No. I use my inner self to deal with the outside world. My life has been guided.

When I listen to my intuition, the universe usually jumps in and helps my decision to be even better. After I have made a decision to follow my intuition, my fears ease up, my anticipation grows, and my new path gets easier and easier.

Be true to yourself. Have integrity with your soul. Often our heads get in the way of our dreams. We must train ourselves to dream like a child and work like an adult to get what we want. Be responsible. I found that confusion is usually the head tackling the heart. Intuition plays a big role in getting what you want. It is a road map. Others will help you along the way, as will the universe. Using intuition is important.

Intuition becomes elevated when in the moments of appreciation. Have you ever needed help and magically someone appeared to help you just at the right moment? Can you remember the feeling you had about them after they were done helping you? It is a feeling of gratefulness, of gratitude, of appreciation. When you think of something to do for them, or to give them because they helped you, your intuition is elevated and helps you think of even nicer ways to show your appreciation, especially where love is concerned.

POINTERS FOR USING YOUR INTUITION:

- Feel more, think less
- It may not make logical sense
- What you feel when someone you love is hurting without being told
- Pay attention to the gnawing feelings inside your stomach
- Work at knowing when using your intuition works for you
- Intuition can be very spontaneous
- Confusion comes from bargaining with the head when we should be listening to the heart
- Reward yourself when you follow your intuition
- Dreams are when you are working things out in your sleep
- Confusion comes when we ignore our intuition
- Intuition works much better when coming from a place of love
- Be true to your self and your soul

One of my mentors Dr. Dollee Campbell taught me a very simple lesson. When it shows up—pay attention to it. The more you use it, the stronger it gets. God said it; I believe it, and that's it. Intuition is meant to help yourself and others around you.

RUTH lives in beautiful Irvine, CA with her husband of seventeen years and four special needs children. She works with great mentors and is now assisting others who are ready for answers and new paths. Ruth is available for consultations, workshops and seminars at (949) 939-0746, mrsruthsanchez@sbcglobal.net. Life experiences: College Graduate, Certified Massage Therapist, Insurance Agent, Miss Bellflower USA 1986, Mrs. Orange County USA 2004, Co-Producer: Your Millionaire Mind, Real Estate Investor, and Gold Congressional Award for Citizens 1985. Visit: www.theaffirmation.com.

CHAPTER 38

Accept Your Goodness Now

ANITA THOMPKINS

PLEASE TAKE A MOMENT right now to "let go" of any notions about who you are, what your purpose is, and any other ideas of yourself that leave you feeling lost. I want you to read this chapter as if your mind was that of a young toddler, open to all the possibilities in the world, believing and absorbing all these words as truth. Accepting what is written as it is. Pure and simple.

I want you to understand how this chapter came to be. About three years ago, I had a terrible accident. As a result, my knee had to be totally reconstructed. Some of you might be thinking, so what? However, when you make your living as a personal trainer, group fitness instructor, nutrition counselor, and a fitness and wellness center owner, it is a huge thing. I was concerned about my recovery, time off, clients, the business, lost income, and the list went on and on. All my life I had defined myself as an "athletic-shaped" woman, and here I was broken. I was scared, lost, and I didn't know who I was. To make matters worse, I was living with my boyfriend and that relationship had major issues.

The surgery occurred in March, 2003. As I lay in the hospital bed with my leg in this contraption that moved it back and forth, I started to cry. The tears were not just from the pain; they were tears that came from deep within my soul. They were the tears not from previous hurts, but from hurts I had done to myself. Hurts from not following my truth and pain for not recognizing that all there is is "God." (When I refer to God, I am referring to whomever you call your higher Presence, the Divine.) My body was broken, but my heart was open, and my intention was very clear. I wanted my life to be completely transformed. It became very clear to me that happiness comes from within, and I realized all the answers were inside of me if I would be quiet, be still, and listen. It took this accident to make me be quiet and still.

During my two weeks at home recuperating, all I could do was sit and listen. Life was happening around me, and there was nothing I could do but know the truth that God was expressing to me on many levels. It was uncomfortable for me to accept there was nothing for me to do except "be," especially since I am an active doer. Sitting still left me in only one place at a time and allowed me to begin living mindfully and peacefully, realizing that my only task in that moment was to "be." I was able to visualize the infinite possibility of my life with no boundaries or limitations set by my own mind. I might have been physically sitting still, but I was moving forward into my divine life.

On April 9, 2003, while still on crutches and facing a year of rehabilitation, I broke up with my boyfriend, moved out and started my journey. On that day, I was ready to accept my goodness. I consciously recognized that there lies within me an Infinite Power and Presence awaiting expression. With this Power and Presence, there is no fear, no challenge, no pain, no strain, and no struggle that cannot be overcome. I realized that "life is good" and that I have the power to create my life. This power is deep within my being, and I am always in a process of creating.

During this two and a half year journey, I have learned and followed these eight guiding principles to create my life. Once I accepted all of these principles deep within my consciousness, my life became full and abundant, and my business grew in ways that I never dreamed.

1. Accept all God has for you so you can express the highest essence of your being. You have to come to a place of awareness where God is all there is. God has given you everything. All is yours; all you have to do is reach out your mental hand and take it.

2. Listen to your truth. Spend at least ten minutes every day in an upright seated posture with your eyes closed and focus on your breathing. This is your quiet, be still time. During these ten minutes, focus only on the inhalation and exhalation of your breathing and nothing else. If your mind wonders with thoughts, bring it back to your breathing. Let the thoughts go and return to focusing on your breathing. Listen to what is being said to you. The voice is small, but it can be heard if you just listen. Meditation is when you are listening for answers. Prayer is when you are asking for things. So meditate more.

3. Be true to yourself and others. Be yourself and enjoy life in your own Divine way. Do not be afraid to be your true self. For everything you want, wants you.

4. Know that you are loved, supported and guided. Come to realize that you are on this earth for a very specific purpose. You are not an accident or just got lucky to survive thus far. You must let go of fear, be open in love and come to know that love supports you. You must know that every step you take is supported and guided by that creative force that moves through you.

5. Release your word and thoughts as law. "As you sow, so shall you reap." Therefore sow the seeds of I am, I can do, and I will do. "As a man thinketh in his heart, so he is." Therefore, think that your life is full beyond measure. Think that your abundance is without limitations and that you are open to all the wonderful experiences that await you.

6. Find your passion. We all make choices. Some choices are great and some are not so great. But don't blame circumstances for your misfortune. Do what you love to do. Whatever it is, just do it and love doing it. Your passion will allow your mind to be free and open your heart and mind to unlimited possibilities.

7. Know what you really want and start creating it. Once you have found your passion then you can start visualizing what you really want for your life. Be sure to know exactly what you wish to produce. You might ask yourself these questions: What do I want for my life? What do I want for my business/job? You must start making these decisions. You don't have to know every detail, but once you start moving on a path to create what you want, the universe will begin to open. Until you are committed, you will experience ineffectiveness and indecisiveness accompanied with wanting to draw back. The moment you definitely commit, then the universe moves too.

8. Be diligent and have the "no matter what" type faith. You must develop the strength of a lion so no matter what, you will stay true to your truth and to your path. This is quite difficult. You will have family and friends who will not understand what you are doing. However, you must stay true to the small voice you heard—your inner you and not be affected by the media, by what you should do according to society, friends or even family.

Live your divine life as it was intended to be, and only you can know that. Develop your lion strength and let it roar.

ANITA is the founder of Thompkins Fitness & Wellness Center where she works one-on-one with clients worldwide to develop long-term habits that supports them in optimal health, fitness and wellness. She empowers clients to change their life from the inside out and assists them in obtaining balance and focus in the mind, body and spirit. How do you rate on the Thompkins scale? Take the quiz and find out. www.anitahasaplanforyou.com. Contact her at (212) 675-6690 or admin@tfwc.us.

ABOUT THE AUTHORS

The women who contributed to this book come from diverse backgrounds and have mastered a wide range of skills and approaches. They are executives, relationship experts, educators, psychotherapists, trainers, doctors, coaches, healers and more. Many have worked for enterprises ranging from Fortune 500 companies to small businesses, though most are now entrepreneurs. The one thing that unites them is success. Every one of them has demonstrated passion and excellence in their endeavors. How can we know this? Results. Though not names you might recognize instantly, many of these women have been featured on national television and in national magazines. They all have something to say worth knowing. Together they have contributed to a book that is greater than the sum of its parts.

ABOUT CHRISTINE KLOSER

Christine Kloser, Author, President of Love Your Life Publishing and Founder of NEW Entrepreneurs, Inc. is an entrepreneur extraordinaire. Christine has coached, advised and inspired thousands of women to take charge of their personal, financial, spiritual and business lives. She is a pioneer in bridging the gap between business and spirituality.

Christine has been a guest on numerous local and national radio and TV shows and her articles and quotes appear in a variety of publications including *Entrepreneur Magazine, Palisadian Post, The Argonaut, She Ink,* and *Woman's Day.* She has also been featured in the books, *What Nobody Ever Tells You About Starting Your Own Business, Web Wonder Women, Heart of a Woman, Visionary Women, Empowering Women to Power Network,* and *Secrets of the Millionaire Mind.* A proud member of the Who's Who of Empowering Executives and Professionals, Christine was also recognized for winning the 2004 Wealthy Woman "Business Ambassador" Award for her dedication to empowering women entrepreneurs.

This book extends the benefits of her creativity and experience to women around the world.

Christine conducts business bi-coastally. She lives in Maryland with her husband and daughter.

To learn more about Christine Kloser, please contact her at:

Christine Kloser
c/o Love Your Life Publishing
PO Box 661274
Los Angeles, CA 90066
Ph: (310) 962-4710
Fax: (310) 496-0716
Email: publish@loveyourlife.com
Web: www.loveyourlife.com

Network for Empowering Women
Helping Women Ignite Their Business And Fuel Their Soul™

Christine Kloser started NEW Entrepreneurs, Inc. in 2000 when she gathered with five friends in the back of a Chinese Restaurant. She had a vision to create a small group of like-minded women who would support each other in entrepreneurial and personal success. That small group has since grown to serve thousands of women world-wide through NEW Connections Ezine, Virtual Meetings, Live Networking Events, Seminars, and most recently our publishing division (Love Your Life Publishing).

You're invited to "get connected" with *NEW Connections Ezine.*

You'll receive FREE Tips, Tools and Resources to turn your "inspirations into realizations!"

NEW Connections is your complete resource for business, spiritual, personal and financial fulfillment.

HERE'S HOW YOU'LL BENEFIT:

- Get invitations to FREE events with leading business and success experts
- Discover resources that save you time and money
- Learn new strategies for boosting your bottom line
- Find out how you can have it all
- And much more

Go to: www.NewNewsletter.com

You'll receive more than $2,000 in bonus gifts, when you subscribe.

Do you have a book inside you?

Most people do.

Just like the contributors to this book, you can see your words in print in six months or less.

Take our short quiz at
www.LoveYourLife.com/authorquiz
to find out if you're ready to get published.

Love Your Life Publishing is your publishing partner, specializing in high quality compilation books.

Love
Your
Life

Love Your Life Publishing
PO Box 661274
Los Angeles, CA 90066
Ph: (310) 962-4710
Fax: (310) 496-0716
Email: publish@loveyourlife.com
Web: www.loveyourlife.com

Also by Love Your Life Publishing:

Stepping Up to the Plate:
Inspiring Interviews with Major Leaguers
By David Kloser
ISBN: 0-9664806-2-7

Inspiration to Realization—Volume I:
Real Women Reveal Proven Strategies for
Personal, Business, Financial and Spiritual Fulfillment
ISBN: 0-9664806-3-5

Love Your Life books may be purchased for educational, business or sales and promotion use.

For information, please write:
Love Your Life Publishing
PO Box 661274
Los Angeles, CA 90066

Email: Publish@loveyourlife.com

Visit: www.loveyourlife.com

Phone: (310) 962-4710